"Heaven and Home":
Charlotte M. Yonge's
Domestic Fiction and the
Victorian Debate
over Women

JUNE STURROCK

"Heaven and Home": Charlotte M. Yonge's Domestic Fiction and the Victorian Debate over Women

English Literary Studies
University of Victoria
1995

ENGLISH LITERARY STUDIES
Published at the University of Victoria

Founding Editor
Samuel L. Macey

GENERAL EDITOR
Robert M. Schuler

EDITORIAL BOARD
Thomas R. Cleary
Evelyn M. Cobley
Kathryn Kerby-Fulton
Victor A. Neufeldt
Stephen A. C. Scobie

ADVISORY EDITORS
David Fowler, *University of Washington*
Donald Greene, *University of Southern California*
Juliet McMaster, *University of Alberta*
Richard J. Schoeck, *University of Colorado*
Arthur Sherbo, *Michigan State University*

BUSINESS MANAGER
Hedy Miller

ISBN 0-920604-84-6

The ELS Monograph Series is published in consultation with members of the Department by ENGLISH LITERARY STUDIES, Department of English, University of Victoria, P.O. Box 3070, Victoria, B.C., Canada, v8w 3w1.

ELS Monograph Series No. 66
© 1995 by June Sturrock

The cover shows a detail from George Richmond's portrait of Charlotte Mary Yonge (1844), © National Portrait Gallery, London. Reproduced by kind permission.

To Katy Rudrum and Sarah Rudrum
and in memory of Ellen May Sturrock
who see and saw the joke

CONTENTS

ACKNOWLEDGMENTS

I am grateful to the Social Sciences and Humanities Research Council of Canada for its financial support. I also wish to thank the librarians of St. Anne's College, Oxford, the English Faculty Library, Oxford, and the Huntington Library for their help. Patricia McClain has been a patient and painstaking research assistant. Friends and colleagues have provided encouragement and helpful suggestions: it is a pleasure to thank Susanna Egan, Mary-Ann Gillies, Juliet McMaster, Kathy Mezei, Betty A. Schellenberg, and especially Alan Rudrum.

A version of Chapter Two appeared in the *Victorian Review*, and I am grateful to the editor for permission to use this material.

ABBREVIATIONS

All the works listed are by Charlotte M. Yonge, unless otherwise indicated. Publication details are given in the list of works cited.

Chaplet	*A Chaplet for Charlotte Yonge.* Ed. Battiscombe and Laski
CWF	*The Clever Woman of the Family*
CY	John Keble, *The Christian Year*
DC	*The Daisy Chain*
DT	*Dynevor Terrace*
FL	Philippa Levine, *Feminist Lives in Victorian England*
JKP	*John Keble's Parishes*
MB	*Magnum Bonum*
Musings	*Musings over "The Christian Year"*
Pillars	*The Pillars of the House*
TSS	*The Two Sides of the Shield*
VF	Philippa Levine, *Victorian Feminism*

PREFACE

One wet Saturday morning years ago I went into a junk shop near Oxford to look for a kitchen chair and came out a few minutes later with ten volumes of the novels of Charlotte Mary Yonge. Jo March in British versions of *Little Women* cries over *The Heir of Redclyffe*, and I was curious to see why she wept. While I was reading (and weeping over) Yonge, my curiosity persisted, first in the form of narrative curiosity, for Yonge is skilled in arousing the urge to know what happens next, and then in the form of curiosity over that narrative curiosity: why should I, why should anyone, care what happened to these pious, prosperous, and unadventurous people? I also wanted to understand more fully the complex implicit and explicit gender codes of these novels, in which a woman's every word or gesture is evaluated according to standards of appropriate femininity. Finally, I was curious about Yonge's certainty, a religious, moral, and social certainty that seemed quite unimaginable. My curiosity about Yonge's religious values and her social assumptions eventually led to the research that is the foundation of this book, which investigates how Yonge's particular brand of antifeminism interacts with her religious beliefs. I begin by setting three novels, one each from the 1850s, the 1860s and the 1870s, in the various contexts of contemporary preoccupations about social change for middle-class women, and then I examine gender in relation to genre, looking at how over a period of twenty-odd years she exploits the potential and expands the capacities of the domestic novel. Although *The Daisy Chain* and *The Clever Woman of the Family* have both been reprinted and a new edition of *The Heir of Redclyffe* is said to be on its way, and despite the appearance of some interesting critical work on Yonge, much of Yonge's fiction has been largely ignored or forgotten. In writing about these novels I share with Jane Spencer the wish that she expressed in relation to her work on earlier novelists—the desire to "contribute to the feminist project of uncovering women's history" (Spencer vii).

INTRODUCTION

"A Daughter of the Church"

"True to the kindred points of heaven and home."
WILLIAM WORDSWORTH, "To a Skylark"

As a favourite phrase of the prolific and best-selling writer, Charlotte Mary Yonge (1823-1901), and one which addresses her double pre-occupation in fiction with "heaven and home," the religious and the domestic, Wordsworth's description of the skylark provides an apt title for this book.[1] In Yonge's novels the middle-class[2] family home is both the central moral arena and the central dramatic arena—the focus of life's most important events. This sense of the significance of events in an environment that was literally familiar, and imaginatively accessible to virtually all her readers, is no doubt one element in Yonge's immense popularity, from the broad appeal of her best-sellers in the 1850s to her continuing wide audience among young women in the 1880s.[3] Yonge's domestic fiction suggests an almost obsessional concern about what it is to be feminine, about what behaviour, language, and concerns are appro-priate for women and what are not, and her definition of femininity is continually revised and restated. This book examines mid-nineteenth-century concepts of gender by looking at three phases of the Victorian debate over women in the light of Yonge's novels of middle-class life and, in an epilogue, by considering the way her imagining of gender roles interacts with her exploitation and re-creation of the domestic novel. All the novels discussed here deal with contemporary life (her historical fiction and works for Sunday School children are ignored) and are drawn from the period of her greatest popularity and productivity, the quarter-century after the publication of the best-selling *The Heir of Redclyffe* in 1853.

Yonge was no feminist; her response to the possibility of social change is invariably conservative. Yet antifeminism is no more unitary than feminism; in the novels discussed in this book, which are evidently written in the context of contemporary debate over issues concerning women, her reaction is never entirely predictable, largely because of her religious and professional position. Any attempt to situate Yonge's fiction historically requires serious consideration not only of gender and class assumptions but also of their interaction with her strong religious concerns and her passion for her own profession. She identified herself strongly as her father's daughter, and thus with social conservatism and the economic interests of the landed gentry, but she also saw herself and projected herself as "a daughter of the church."[4] Her religious convictions, formed first by her father's High Church teachings and later by John Keble's Tractarianism, drove her to reject certain "worldly" values —some of the common values of her gender, class, and period—and this rejection of the worldly complicates at all stages her response to social change. She supported on principle what Mill called "the despotism of custom" (Brian Harrison 27), in accordance with the Tractarian reverence for establishment, hierarchy, and tradition, and she valued existing situations, structures, relationships and behaviours as part of a providential disposition.

Yet her concern with the spiritual life, and above all the understanding of work as evidence of spiritual health that grew from a combination of the Tractarian emphasis on "good works" and her personal experience of absorption in her own work, led to a foregrounding of aspects of female life beyond the erotic and the domestic, so that many of the concerns of less conservative contemporary women, such as education, work, and political and social change, were also inescapably her concerns. Marriage is important in many of her novels: *The Three Brides* (discussed in Chapter Three) is largely a disquisition on women's marital obligations, for instance. Yet her novels rarely (arguably never) move towards marriage as resolution, and despite her admiration for the work of Jane Austen and her use of Austen's work as a model,[5] none of Yonge's novels could be described as "marriage novels." While her women characters usually define themselves in relation to men, the dominant relationship may well be that of father and daughter (as with Ethel and Dr. May in *The Daisy Chain*), or sister and brother (as with Geraldine and Felix in *The Pillars of The House*, or (female) guardian and (male) ward (as with Honora and Owen in *Hopes and Fears*), rather than that of lovers or of husband and wife. And while embracing domestic responsibilities, Yonge's women are likely also to look beyond those responsibilities for their vocations, as workers for charity, as responsible land-owners, writers, painters, or teachers.

Stephen Prickett contends that in nineteenth-century England innovations were "as much products of attempts to defend an existing position as of efforts consciously to create change" (182). Yonge certainly does not work towards social change for women, but she does attempt to understand the changing position of women in her period, and she accepts change once it has happened as being in its turn providential, the new status quo to which a good Christian must be resigned. The following introduction outlines three issues that relate to her changing understanding of the feminine and the masculine: her own life and work, especially her devotion to her father and to her own profession; her Tractarianism, especially her relationship with Keble and those tenets of his that most affected her work; and her interaction with the "woman question," the discussion of which as a general issue is necessarily limited for the purposes of this book.[6]

I

In examining Yonge's domestic novels in the context of the contemporary debate over women I inevitably address the questions Beth Kowaleski-Wallace has asked about two earlier women writers, Hannah More and Maria Edgeworth, whose work Yonge respected and who, like Yonge, firmly identify themselves as "their fathers' daughters": "What does it mean for a woman writer to identify with her father and with the patriarchal tradition he represents? What factors . . . motivate such identification? What are the consequences of this identification?" (vii). Partial answers to these large questions will emerge below. Meanwhile it is perhaps adequate merely to assert that she did indeed identify herself strongly as her "father's daughter"; as Dennis points out Yonge, despite her evident affection for her mother, identified exclusively with her father's family (8). She depended throughout her father's life on her sense of his approval: she wrote in a late autobiographical fragment that "his approbation was throughout life my bliss; his anger my misery for the time" (Romanes 16). Obviously such dependence was emotionally and perhaps intellectually costly. Her longing for his good opinion apparently arose as much from fear as from love. She writes, for instance, of the arithmetic lessons that he gave her first as a child:

> He thundered at me so that nobody could bear to hear it, and often reduced me to tears, but his approbation was so delightful that it was a delicious stimulus . . . I believe, in spite of all breezes over my innate slovenliness, it would have broken our hearts to leave off working together. And we went on till I was some years past twenty.   (Coleridge 108)

But of course for Yonge and her father fear was an appropriate response to a parent and especially to a father. Like some other writers of her period she thought in terms of the fifth commandment, "honour thy father and thy mother," and as a Tractarian especially she was committed to obedience to established authority, including the traditional family hierarchy. Yonge frequently writes as if the wish to please one's father is a

17

prime motive in life. For instance, she advises educators thus: "let the children feel that every step in learning renders them more companionable to their father, and he will do more for them than is in the power of any other creature" (*Womankind* 29). The father, that is, does not actively teach; this is the province of the mother or governess. However, he inspires the child to learn through his position of power.

The deepest relationship in Yonge's "uneventful life"[7] seems to have been this strong dependence on her father. This experience dominates her imagination and presumably colours her versions of gender relations. As a matter of principle she advocates extreme filial obedience in her writings;[8] the implicit obedience due even a debauched father is a repeated motif in her novels (*Dynevor Terrace, The Three Brides, Nuttie's Father*). However, she also foregrounds the extreme power of filial affection. When a widowed father expresses unhappiness at the engagement of his daughter, another daughter reacts by silently and entirely dedicating her life to him:

> Ethel stood unnoticed and silent, making no outward protestation, but with lips compressed, as in her heart of hearts, she passed the resolution — that her father should never feel this pain [the pain of a daughter's intended marriage] on her account. Leave him who might, she would never forsake him. Nothing but the will of Heaven should part them. It might be hasty and venturesome. She knew not what it might cost her; but . . . she . . . laid up her secret vow — that no earthly object should be placed between her and her father. (*DC* 393)

And indeed she eventually gives up, with little serious regret, the chance of a happy and suitable marriage, as well as her personal freedom, for the sake of lifelong devotion to her father. Yonge's fictional marriages often seem to be imagined in terms of such intense father-daughter relationships. When a newly-engaged eighteen-year-old first kisses her thirty-five-year-old husband-to-be, her comment is "it was like when papa kissed me before he went away" (*Magnum Bonum* 13), and in the ensuing marriage she is treated more like a petted eldest daughter than a responsible adult. Similarly in *The Clever Woman of the Family* (discussed in Chapter Two) when the sixteen-year-old Fanny marries a sixty-year-old soldier, she is said to exist in a "prolonged childhood" (24), "tended like an infant by her bustling mother and doting husband" (5), despite the seven children she rapidly bears "the chivalrous old man" (24). Such marriages, which abound in these novels,[9] must be read in the context of the period: Yonge's contemporaries, notably Dickens, also occasionally blurred the distinctions between marital and filial relationships (for instance in the

Strongs' marriage in *David Copperfield*). All the same, filial relationships dominate Yonge's imagination, and this fact inevitably affects her understanding of gender relationships. Yonge seems to have understood herself as being above all a loving and obedient daughter, and she interpreted other relationships in these terms.

Yonge's devotion to her father and her need for his approval was avowedly a driving motive, but her need to write was equally urgent: when asked what she would have done if her father had forbidden her to publish, she promptly replied, "Oh I must have written; but I should never have published, at least not for many years" (Coleridge 153). Writing, like her father's approbation, was a matter of emotional necessity for her: the most important negotiation of Yonge's life, therefore, was between these two needs, her compulsion to write and the need to avoid the disapproval of a controlling and conservative parent. Near the end of her life she wrote about this crisis in relation to the publication of her first full novel, *Abbey Church*, in 1844 when she was twenty-one years old:[10]

> I cannot forget . . . my father, before taking any steps about Abbey Church, gravely putting it before me that there were three reasons for which one might desire to publish—love of vanity, or of gain, or the wish to do good. I answered, with tears, that I really hoped I had written with the purpose of being useful to young girls like myself. The matter of gain we were old-fashioned enough to hold as quite out of the question; and for a long time it was a point of honour, and perhaps of duty with me to spend none of it on myself. ("Lifelong Friends," *Chaplet* 183)

Showalter comments that "by doing good and taking no pay she was safely confined in a female and subordinate role and remained dependent upon her father" (*Literature* 56-57); this comment is perhaps just in relation to Yonge's father, but for Yonge herself her tearful answer provided her with both the emotional and the economic freedom that she needed to pursue a demanding literary career and to work extremely hard at it for the rest of a long life. She consistently speaks of the professional life thus opened to her as both pleasure and vocation; in old age she writes that at the age of thirty, after the success of *The Heir of Redclyffe* (which, incidentally, preceded the death of her father by barely a year), "authorship ceased . . . to be a simple amusement, and became a vocation, though never less of a delight, and I hope I may say, of a conscience" ("Lifelong Friends," *Chaplet* 184). Certainly a greater complexity is perceptible in her work from this point onwards, as well as a professional confidence that for the first time allowed her to listen to advice "with deference and gratitude" but to take "none of it" (Coleridge

19

166). Her relish for her work, the "delight" she speaks of, is apparent in her own correspondence and that of her friends and family, which is full of news and gossip about Yonge's characters. Her mother wrote to a friend: "I think Charlotte is the one person who has more pleasure from her books than I have. We never tire of talking of them before they are written and correcting the MS and the proofs" (Mare and Percival 143), and in the mid-1890s Yonge was still eagerly chatting about her latest batch of characters.[11]

In her compulsion to write, Yonge managed to associate vocation, delight, and a sensitive conscience by focusing on the didactic function of her novels so that she came to describe her professional self as "a sort of instrument for popularizing Church views that might not otherwise have been taken in" (Romanes 190). She continued to liberate herself emotionally for her work by viewing it as "written with the purpose of being useful," as she had told her father; that negotiation with patriarchal power continued long after his death. In mid-career she advises aspiring women writers that "the rule of only writing as a Christian, with the glory of God in view, needs to be kept in mind. . . . Authorship must never be viewed as a mere trade for gaining money" (*Womankind* 228): they should write, that is, as she does. She was apparently aware of the critical ridicule to which she became open because of her determined didacticism. In one of her later novels, which touches on the responsibilities of authorship, a foolish beginning writer comments that "the critics always laugh at things with a purpose"; but a more mature and successful colleague responds, "I don't think that is a reason for not trying to do good even in this very small and uncertain way" (*TSS* 2.158).[12] Yonge consistently and insistently presents her own writing to herself and to her readers as "trying to do good."

Yonge led an astonishingly active professional life. Not only did she write about two hundred independent works ranging from novels of contemporary life to historical textbooks and other schoolbooks, to children's books for various social classes,[13] to serious biographies, like that of Bishop Coleridge Patteson, and to works of topography and etymology,[14] but she also provided stories and articles for periodicals such as *Macmillan's Magazine* and *The Magazine for the Young*. In addition, she occasionally acted as Macmillan's reader for religious manuscripts (Tuchman 72), all the while working as editor of various Church journals: *Mothers in Council* (1890-1901), *The Monthly Paper of Sunday School Teaching* (1860-75), and especially the periodical with which her name was always associated, *The Monthly Packet* (1850-90; co-editor 1890-99)

(Coleridge 368). She was one of the many women of the period who shared a degree of power within the literary world. As Mermin says, "the most prestigious journals that printed new literary works were edited by men . . . but women could be editors too, particularly of journals for women and children, or, like Geraldine Jewsbury, exercise similar power as publishers' readers" (*Godiva's Ride* 44).[15] Conservative women apparently felt as free to exercise this power as their more liberal sisters. Charlotte Elizabeth Tonna, for instance, a less successful Evangelical version of the Tractarian Yonge, published novels and also acted as editor to the *Christian Ladies' Magazine, Protestant Annual,* and *Protestant Magazine* (Krueger 130). Indeed the literary was apparently the most popular profession for middle-class women.[16] While Yonge's concepts of gender were necessarily modified by her own experience, her professional role as such did not necessarily challenge the gender ideology of her father's daughter.[17]

II

Yonge's most significant literary relationship was her close and quasi-filial friendship with one of the best-known religious writers of her period. John Keble came to take over the parishes of Hursley and Otterbourne, the Yonge family's home, as their vicar in 1835 when Yonge was twelve years old. He was by then already known for his association with the movement for renewal within the Anglican church that was to be variously labeled Tractarianism, the Oxford Movement, or Puseyism; the Assize Sermon on National Apostasy, which he had preached on July 14, 1833 in the University Church in Oxford, marked the real beginning of the movement, according to John Henry Newman, who saw Keble as its "true and primary author" (590). Tractarianism began in angry reaction to the liberalising reforms of the 1830s and the rationalism and secularism on which these reforms were based. "Speak I must," writes Newman at the beginning of the first of the *Tracts for the Times* (those tracts which gave the movement one of its names), "for the times are very evil, yet no one speaks against them" (Church 112). For the next twelve years Keble, Newman, Edward Pusey, Isaac Williams, and others spoke out pugnaciously against the evils of the times, and when these twelve years of active debate were ended by Newman's defection to Rome—"the great sorrow of [Keble's] life," according to Yonge (*JKP* 114)—Tractarianism continued to ferment within English social and religious life, activated partly by the popular work of Charlotte Yonge.

21

In 1835, then, Keble was known as a religious controversialist; but he was far better known as a religious poet. *The Christian Year,* "a collection of devotional verses based on the services of the Anglican *Book of Common Prayer*" (*CY* xi), published in 1827, was for years generally regarded as, in Newman's words, "one of the classics of the language" (591). It went through ninety-five editions in Keble's life time, and on the basis of its success Keble was elected Professor of Poetry at Oxford (1831-41). His parishioners were therefore aware that their new vicar was a distinguished man, and Keble's educated and pious conservatism, and his idiosyncratic combination of humility and unbending dogmatism, suited well with the Yonges, who gave him full cooperation and warm friendship. After Keble's arrival, Yonge remembers, "the new state of things was soon felt. Daily services and monthly Eucharists began; and the school teaching and cottage visiting were full of new life" (*JKP* 99). Keble, that is, established immediately his religious priorities: the services of the *Book of Common Prayer,* the sacraments, charitable works, and education. His educational activities necessarily included giving confirmation classes to the adolescents of the neighbourhood, and in this way his religious views began to have a direct effect on his bright young parishioner: "at fifteen," Yonge records, "I became a catechumen of Mr. Keble and this I would call the greatest influence of my life" (*Musings* iii). This influence she describes elsewhere as "not so much friendly as fatherly," and she acknowledges Keble with "thankfulness too deep to be spoken," not only for his religious teaching and personal affection but also for his help as "the best and kindest critic in literary affairs" (*JKP* 140). Yonge met Newman (*JKP* 105) and Pusey (Mare and Percival 218) only briefly; it was from Keble, its founder, that she imbibed her particular version of Tractarianism, a Tractarianism that strongly colours her views of gender. Keble's example and his words resound throughout her work: his stated aim in *The Christian Year* of bringing readers' "thoughts and feelings into more entire unison with those recommended and exemplified in the Prayer Book" (*CY* 1) is closely echoed in Yonge's own statement of didactic intent in the preface to the first number of the young women's magazine she would edit for decades, *The Monthly Packet*:

> Above all, it is the especial desire and prayer of those who address you through the pages of this magazine that what you find there may tend to make you more steadfast and dutiful daughters of our own beloved Catholic Church of England, and may go alongside in all respects with the teaching, both doctrinal and practical, of the Prayer Book. (Romanes 47)

Their common insistence on their work's fundamental relationship to the *Book of Common Prayer* shows an essential feature of the religious doctrine that Yonge and Keble shared. A Tractarian bases "acceptance of the Holy Word, not only on its internal evidence, but on the authority of the Church, which he can distinctly prove," according to Yonge (*Womankind* 215).[18] Thus, unlike more avowedly Protestant Christians, Tractarians necessarily depend less on the independent workings of the individual conscience, which necessarily modifies biblical interpretation by "internal evidence," and more on a rigid interpretive and liturgical tradition; they therefore eschew change and aim to live in obedience to established hierarchies, most explicitly ecclesiastical hierarchies, but also the political and social orders. Keble's Tractarian teaching thus reinforced the Yonge family code in important ways that clearly relate to the position of women in the middle-class family, so that issues such as matrimonial law reform or women's suffrage would necessarily be suspect; in her writings Yonge explicitly rejects such proposed changes (see Chapter Three).

The Yonges' support of existing family structures was further reinforced by Keble's beliefs and personal example. To him as to them the filial tie was preeminent; he had given up his own successful career as an Oxford fellow to tend a rural parish and look after his aging father: "he had turned from the admiration which haunted his steps, and sought for a better and holier satisfaction," according to Newman (591). Yonge's sense of the preeminence of private and domestic satisfactions as opposed to public success, which affects both how she understands gender and how she works with the domestic novel (as discussed in my epilogue), thus parallel Keble's belief in and practice of self-effacement. Societal expectations commonly associated self-effacement and self-sacrifice with the feminine; Keble's version of Christianity reinforced but also generalized feminine and domestic virtues. In Keble's Tractarianism, then, behaviour associated with the feminine and the domestic became prescribed more generally as Christian behaviour.

Keble's insistence on modesty and humility as requisite Christian virtues was also by no means gender specific. When he warned Yonge after the publication of *The Heir of Redclyffe* that "a successful book might be the trial of one's life" (Mare and Percival 139), he clearly had his own similar experience with *The Christian Year* in mind. Keble wrote in praise of a religious reticence that "fears in open day to shine" (*CY* 34), and quoted with approval a comment on the seventeenth-century Lord Chief Justice who carefully concealed his religious feelings "not only in obedience of the rule given by our Saviour . . . but from a particular distrust he had of himself" (*CY* 34). Keble believed in the value of reserve and privacy: "Why should gentle hearts and true / Bare to the rude world's withering view / Their treasure of delight?" (*CY* 57). Again the feminine position of avoidance of the public realm—"the rude world"—and devotion to the private realm was generalized and seen as a Christian virtue rather than a gender-specific virtue. Keble's pupil's later celebrations of the domestic must be seen in the context of these religious beliefs as well as of gender codes.

Keble's Tractarian insistence on the role of charity—of "good works" —in the religious life operates rather differently in relation to Yonge's views of gender (her treatment of women and work is discussed in Chapter Two). He believed that through good actions a Christian can come to spiritual health, that charity is "the life of faith" (*CY* vii). In emphasizing the significance of good works, Tractarians differentiated themselves from Low Church Evangelicals, who believed in salvation through faith alone. Keble lived according to his beliefs, constantly active in "teaching in the school, catechising in the church, most carefully preparing for confirmation, watching over the homes and, however otherwise busied, always at the beck and call of everyone in the parish" (*JKP* 140). For Yonge, with her personal experience of the efficacy of work, this teaching was undoubtedly palatable, and she repeatedly presents her women characters as craving work, as working effectively, and as developing in faith through their work.

In her study of the origins of modern feminism, Rendall suggests that "religious factors were of vital importance in explaining the development of association amongst women and the growth of that moralising force— whether religious or secular—which is so strong a feature of women's action by the mid-nineteenth century" (322). Despite Yonge's antifeminism, her work may justly be read in the context of this juxtaposition of religion, women's action, and their moralizing force. Certainly she is sharply critical of "women's rights" workers and women who ignore their obvious (i.e., familial) duties; undoubtedly she is conservative in her fundamentalist view of the subordination of women as proper for the daughters of Eve ("I have no hesitation in declaring my full belief in the inferiority of woman, nor that she brought it upon herself" [*Womankind* 1-2], she writes, and proceeds to claim "that there is this [intellectual] inequality there is no reasonable doubt"). Yet her religious views compelled her, and her own work encouraged her, to think of women's activities as a serious issue, and to question many of the traditional activities and criteria of middle-class women. No doubt Tractarianism

24

had a less dramatic effect on Yonge's sense of gender relations than on Christina Rossetti's, which Anthony Harrison sees in terms of

> a quietly comprehensive attack on the entire network of patriarchal values which even the most stringent social critics of her day normally accept without question. Surprisingly, and it may seem, paradoxically, Rossetti is able to accomplish this goal by positioning herself as a devout adherent of High Anglican religious doctrine, and, ostensibly, as an advocate of the more widespread Victorian ideology of "woman's sphere." By embracing religious values with a uniquely radical fervour, however, Rossetti's work undercuts the domestic ideology of middle-class and upper-class Victorians, and functions to subvert both the patriarchal values that governed Victorian England and their extension in industrial capitalism. (89)

McGann, too, speaks of Rossetti's "open confrontation with 'the world'" (5). Yonge's challenge to contemporary values is more modest than that of her brilliant contemporary and operates quite differently. Rather than undercutting domestic ideology, she actually extends it far beyond its conventional limitations and represents the domestic—and by implication, the feminine—as morally, spiritually, and culturally central for male as well as female. She moralizes and thus universalizes the home.

The foregrounding of the domestic is, of course, a commonplace of the period, and some of the most outspoken feminist leaders can sound curiously close to Yonge here. For example, Josephine Butler, the leader of the movement for repeal of the Contagious Diseases Acts,[19] carefully establishes her own enthusiatic commitment to the domestic: "Home is the nursery of all virtues, the fountainhead of all the affections, and the main source of the strength of our nation" (xxv).[20] Butler's colleague, Frances Power Cobbe, similarly describes domesticity without apparent irony as "this overpowering force" (12). For such essayists their view of the domestic must remain a matter of assertion. Yonge, however, as a novelist can define and demonstrate the domestic through the imagined interactions of her domestic fiction: she can show the domestic as the supreme masculine as well as the supreme feminine quality, and portray those women who are most committed to domesticity as also committed to work.

Generally speaking, Yonge's religious beliefs both broaden and restrict her range. They provide her with a base from which to challenge certain conventions, and to see that respectability was not the supreme moral virtue (for instance, one of her good clergymen is "quite disheartened and disgusted by the respectability" of his parish [DT 390]). Yet they also inhibit her writing. Elizabeth Langland has argued of one of

Yonge's contemporaries that because "she is committed to a truly moral life and not merely a socially proper or correct life Anne Brontë presents a radical critique of Victorian society" (126). Yonge, similarly activated by religious fervour, presents a critique of Victorian society from a unique point of view: but her critique is less open and direct than Brontë's, partly because of the relation between her religious beliefs and her concepts of gender. One aspect of Keble's teaching that Yonge accepted apparently without question was his insistence on extreme "delicacy" over physical and especially sexual matters, so that for instance novels that are full of births are almost entirely lacking in pregnancies,[21] and any vice or debauchery that is necessary for the plot is not only off-stage but non-specific. In virtually all of Yonge's novels women characters express a feeling of oppression at the demands of feminine propriety,[22] but their author willingly takes on an extreme of novelistic propriety that made her notorious in her own lifetime. For a contemporary commentator on the contrasts among women writers, "the authoress of 'the Heir of Redclyffe'" was the natural antithesis of George Sand (Cobbe 6).[23] Yonge's insistence on observing the feminine conventions was in its own way as conspicuous as Sand's relish in flouting them.

III

"Of all the theories current concerning women, none is more curious than the theory that it is needful to make a theory about them," according to the feminist writer, Frances Power Cobbe, commenting in 1869 on the endless investigations of the nature of the feminine that characterize this period (1).[24] Yonge's explicit "theory" about women as such is largely confined to the pages of *Womankind*, her book of essays, and her editorializing for *The Monthly Packet*, but her novels show an endless engagement with the subject of proper femininity. *The Daisy Chain* (discussed in Chapter One), for instance, is full of implied or asserted distinctions between the feminine and the masculine (usually Ethel and Norman) and the sincerely and the falsely feminine (usually Ethel and Flora). *The Clever Woman of the Family* (discussed in Chapter Two) can be read as a protracted investigation of the properly feminine intellect and its appropriate employment. *The Three Brides* (see Chapter Three) looks at the appropriate feminine approach to both the public and the private realm. Yonge writes mainly of women and mainly for women: not only was *The Monthly Packet* directed principally and dogmatically at women of about fifteen to twenty-five years of age — "it became indeed a Maidens' Manual" (Coleridge 165) — but her novels, too, once the initial impact of *The*

Heir of Redclyffe had worn off, drew mainly on a female readership. Ethel Romanes, her younger friend, observes that Yonge "wrote mainly for women. Her earlier books undoubtedly had a certain amount of popularity among men; but so far as she had any sense of mission, we are sure she thought only of her own sex" (176). Nicola Thompson, discussing ideas of gender and the reception of mid-nineteenth-century fiction, comments at length on how closely Yonge conformed in *The Heir of Redclyffe* to the contemporary ideal of the feminine writer, and how positively this perceived femininity affected the reception of her work (190-228).[25] The comments of both Romanes and Thompson indicate Yonge's especially developed sensitivity to the issue of gender, a sensitivity which she cultivated because of the connections that she perceived between the construction of gender and her religion. Her special curiosity about these issues led her increasingly to engage in the debate about Victorian women, as I shall show in the following pages, attempting not so much to identify precisely how Yonge reacts to this debate as to show the texts in question as a peculiar part of the discourse of gender of the period.

The women's movement of the nineteenth century worked on many levels and engaged with many causes, according to Philippa Levine, who proceeds to argue, however, that "feminists did not displace their energies by severing their politics into an abundance of single issue campaigns, but rather used those several campaigning questions" (*FL* 176-79). Feminist campaigns in Yonge's life times moved in various directions. For this discussion, I adopt the hypothesis of three stages of activity and debate: first, in the 40s and 50s, a focus on women's education; second, in the 50s and 60s, a concern with women's limited employment options; and third, after 1867, an emphasis on legal and political freedoms. Of course this is to some extent a convenient fiction: concern with women's education did not disappear in the 1860s any more than arguments over women's political position began in 1867. Moreover, important campaigns, like that over the repeal of the Contagious Diseases Acts, are omitted from the discussion, as they were from Yonge's representation of society.

Yet my hypothesis bears some resemblance to the less tidy progress of actual events. The career of the feminist Barbara Leigh Smith Bodichon (1827-1891) can be seen as moving through the three stages discussed here, for in the early 1850s she devoted much of her energy to education, opening an experimental school in London in 1856, while in the early 1860s with the Langham Place group and the Society for Providing Employment for Women she concentrated on women and work; in the late 1860s her attention was directed towards the issue of suffrage, which for some years she saw as the key issue for women.[26] My argument is that as the debate generally shifted its focus from education to employment to politics and the law, so did Yonge's work. Yonge, the antifeminist, engages with the issues that troubled the feminists of her day, obliquely at first, but increasingly more openly and strongly. Each chapter that follows therefore discusses in some detail one novel from each period: *The Daisy Chain* in relation to education, *The Clever Women of the Family* in relation to employment, and *The Three Brides* in relation to political and legal reforms. Other novels are treated more briefly in passing. The conclusion, rather than focusing on one novel and one period, moves into a wider focus, to allow an overview of the relation between Yonge's understanding of gender codes and her use of the genre of domestic fiction.

CHAPTER ONE

"A Regular Learned Lady":
The Daisy Chain (1856)
and Educational Reform

The Daisy Chain begins in the May family's schoolroom, complete with desks, piano, globe, and loaded bookshelves, and never moves completely away from the world of education. Market Stoneborough, the country town in which the novel is set, is notable only for the endowed grammar school which the May boys attend, and except for a brief excursion to Oxford, for the University's commemoration ceremonies, the narrative hardly leaves Stoneborough.[1] The daisy chain of the title is formed by the eleven May children, who are at various stages of their education during the course of the novel and who function as teachers as well as students, for they not only teach in the parish Sunday School but also found a school for the poor and illiterate children of a nearby hamlet. At the end of the novel two of the main characters go off to New Zealand as missionary and wife to teach the Maoris and settlers there. All through her career Yonge wrote about education, especially the education of young middle-class women, but in no other work is the subject as central as in this self-styled "family chronicle" of the mid-1850s, which deals with the education not only of middle-class girls but also of their brothers and their working-class neighbours.[2]

In *The Daisy Chain*, a novel intensely concerned with issues of gender and education, Yonge is writing in the context of a new surge of interest in women's education that would form a vital preliminary stage to the development of the woman's movement of the nineteenth century—what Levine calls "the first step" (*VF* 7) towards equal rights. The specific interest in the education of middle-class women evident in the 1840s and 50s is part of a more general nation-wide concern with educational reform for both sexes and all classes, especially among Tractarians like Yonge. The reforms affecting middle-class girls and women tended to take them out of the home, the traditional setting for their education, and place them in institutions; the changes affecting boys and men involved new institutions or changes in traditional institutions, both in curriculum and in moral training. My discussion begins with an outline of the changes in women's education during the 1840s and 50s, notes specifically Tractarian work towards educational reform, and goes on to discuss *The Daisy Chain* in this context, focusing especially on its treatment of the relation between gender and education, and showing how Yonge connects ideals of both the feminine and the masculine in education to the ideology of the private sphere, the consecration of the home. While Yonge presents learning as a pleasure for women as well as for men, religious, social, and domestic usefulness, rather than public success, is the ultimate value for both sexes. I also deal, though more briefly, with *The Trial* (1864), a sequel to *The Daisy Chain*, in which Yonge elaborates on both the ideology of home and the idea of education in relation to class and gender.

I

After its initial success, Mary Wollstonecraft's eloquent argument for the necessity of women's education in *A Vindication of the Rights of Women* (1792) probably had a negative rather than a positive effect on her cause, and for many years the education of women was virtually forgotten.[3] Working women were often virtually illiterate, and many middle-class women were not much more advanced (Taylor 232). One fictitious and two real institutions for the higher education of women brought this issue to the general attention in the late 1840s. The fictitious institution was the women-only university founded by Princess Ida in Tennyson's *The Princess* (1847); the real institutions were Queen's College, London, opened in 1848, and Bedford College, London, opened in 1849. While the Princess's university was based on male fantasies of a woman's dream of a college where students can "lose the child, assume / The woman" (136-37),[4] the real colleges arose immediately from a concern with the education of middle-class women as a practical means rather than an end in itself.

Governesses at this period were both poorly paid and poorly trained, so that employers and employees alike were frequently dissatisfied with each other. One obvious if partial solution was to train these women so that their performance might improve and thus gain them greater respect and higher salaries. The patrons of the Governesses' Benevolent Institution, founded in 1843 to provide financial help to "ladies in temporary distress" (Strachey 60), included Mary Maurice. Her brother, Frederick Denison Maurice, had early demonstrated his interest in women's education with a "slashing attack" on existing girls' schools in 1825

(Killham 73), and together with Charles Kingsley, his colleague at King's College, London, he responded to the urgent problem by offering a series of lectures for girls and women which were the beginning of Queen's College. The unexpected success of this venture presumably encouraged Elizabeth Reid, the next year, in opening Bedford College, a woman-run and non-denominational version of the male-run Anglican Queen's College, with lecturers from the non-denominational University College rather than the Anglican King's College.[5]

Not only governesses but other women and girls were eager to take advantage of these new opportunities, for lack of education was not merely an occupational concern for prospective teachers, but a wider problem for women hungry for skills and knowledge or parents anxious about their daughters' ignorance. Before the 1840s middle-class women were usually dependent on half-educated mothers, sisters, governesses, or small schools with low academic standards for their education; this situation did not change rapidly, but by the 1840s public support for change was noticeably growing.[6] The *Westminster Review* claimed in 1841 that "on the subject of [women's] education public opinion and practice have undergone a complete change within a very few years" (Killham 125). As Rendall argues, "by the 1840s the climate of opinion had shifted towards recognition of the extremely poor standard of education offered to middle-class girls" (132); the colleges were a necessary early step in improving standards.

Another educational opening seized on by middle-class women in the 1840s was provided by the residential colleges established between 1839 and 1846 to train teachers, both men and women, for the new elementary schools, providing courses that varied from three months to three years. The popularity of these colleges among leisured women, like the extraordinary success of the London colleges, indicated dissatisfaction with previously tolerated standards of middle-class women's education. These colleges were not intended for the prosperous middle-classes — elementary school teachers had little social prestige and usually came from lower middle-class backgrounds — but by 1851 ten per cent of the women entrants were from wealthier, professional families. The decline in the proportion of middle-class entrants after that date (Rendall 133) indicates perhaps the existence of more appropriate facilities elsewhere.

In the subsequent development of women's education the two new London colleges for women played the key role, especially in the foundation of the new high schools for girls which opened in the 1850s: the first women to organize schools for middle-class girls with similar goals to the public schools for boys came from Queen's College and Bedford College (Burstyn 24), and included Dorothea Beale, Frances Buss, Sophia Jex-Blake, and Barbara Leigh Smith. The North London Collegiate School was opened in 1850, and Cheltenham Ladies' College in 1854; both were schools for middle-class girls, stressing academic education rather than more traditional feminine lore, whether accomplishments, such as music and embroidery (*VF* 39) or housewifery (*VF* 54). In 1854 Barbara Leigh Smith opened Portman Hall School, a more experimental institution in that it enrolled both boys and girls, and children from prosperous middle-class families as well as the children of local workers and trades people (Herstein 62), and emphasized intellectual understanding rather than rote learning. The varied agendas of the educational reformers are also shown in the publications on the subject of women's education at this period, such as Harriet Martineau's *Household Education* (1849), F. D. Maurice's *Queen's College, London, Its Objects and Method* (1848), Maria Grey and Emily Shirreff's *Thoughts on Self-Culture Addressed to Women* (1850), and Bessie Rayner Parkes's *Remarks on the Education of Girls*. Grey and Shirreff, for instance, see educational improvements as equipping women to be better wives, while Parkes thinks in terms of total equality. The common demand among reformers of various shades of opinion, however, was for more and better educational institutions for girls and young women of all classes.

After the 1850s came a temporary lull in the reform of women's education (*VF* 34), no doubt partly because many active and articulate women turned their attention to the need for more varied employment opportunities for women, as discussed in my next chapter. But of course the reform of women's education once begun did not cease, and in the later years of the century many more new high schools were founded, women's colleges opened at Oxford and Cambridge, and the Girls' Public Day Schools Trust was organized. But the first burst of energy came in the 1840s and 50s.

II

Educational reform at this period emerges as a manifestation of the growing power of the middle-class: existing forms of education, for middle-class boys as well as for girls, were perceived as inappropriate to the changing needs of that class. Education was an especially important issue to the Tractarians, whose insistence on ecclesiastical, cultural, and political traditions after all implied the need for schooling in these traditions. As Ollard, the historian of the Oxford Movement, points out, "the first men of the Oxford Movement were scholars and teachers; it was natural therefore that education should be quickened and enriched by their work" (167). The best-known of the many Tractarians working in education is Nathaniel Woodard, the author of *A Plea for the Middle Classes* (1848) and *Public Schools for the Middle Classes* (1852), which argue that public school education, a privilege offered to too few, should be made more accessible, and that other schools, operating on Anglican "prayer-book" principles, should be established. Woodard acted on his own suggestions: he started up a day school with two staff members in his own dining room in 1847 (Heeney, *Mission* 22), and his two best-known schools were founded at this period, Hurstpierpoint in 1853 and Lancing in 1857.[7] Several other Woodard schools were opened later, including schools for girls, such as St. Michael's, Worthing, and St. Mary's, Abbot's Bromley, despite his objections to "fancy schools for girls" based on his view that "we all know what women are for" (Heeney, *Mission* 107).

During the same period, many of Yonge's friends and acquaintances were able to emphasize the educational role of the church through their work in long-established institutions. Both Harrow and Winchester, for example, were headed for long periods by men who aligned themselves with the Oxford Movement: Harrow by Christopher Wordsworth (later Bishop of Lincoln), the father of Elizabeth Wordsworth, Yonge's friend and the first principal of Lady Margaret Hall, Oxford; and Winchester by George Moberly (later Bishop of Salisbury), the father of Charlotte Moberly, first Principal of St. Hugh's Hall, Oxford. (Moberly's younger daughter, Margaret, was Yonge's godchild, after whom all the four Margarets of *The Daisy Chain* are named.) One of Yonge's constant correspondents was the sister-in-law of W. J. Butler, the priest in charge of the Sisterhood of St. Mary the Virgin, Wantage, a community with an educational mission to all social classes. Marianne Dyson, who gave Yonge the plot of *The Heir of Redclyffe*, was arguably "the first pioneer of middle-class education for girls. She set up a boarding school for superior village girls" (Coleridge 147), and "for these Charlotte wrote *The Chosen People* and *Kings of England*" (Romanes 44), the first of dozens of books by Yonge intended for classrooms and schoolrooms.[8] Given such a strong link between Tractarianism and education it is not surprising that after the death of Keble, according to Yonge's own account, his "most fitting memorial" was felt to be "the building of the college at Oxford which bears his name and is pledged to Church principles and to a scale of expenses not beyond the reach of less wealthy students" (*JKP* 144). Tractarian educational reforms were based on their belief in the need for greater access to education that provided schooling in church traditions.

Thus at a time of change and debate concerning education, and especially the education of women, Yonge produces *The Daisy Chain*, a novel that concentrates on education to the extent that learning and teaching might seem the primary activities in life for women and men alike. If Yonge's interest in education is merely an intensification of a preoccupation that is typical of her period, her educational priorities nevertheless provide an implicit critique of current trends in education for both boys and girls.[9] The establishment of the new colleges and schools is evidence of the movement towards institutionalizing the education of women, moving it out of the home and making it less a part of family life. In Yonge's novel, by contrast, the home is central and a woman's education is largely related to her home duties. Yet Yonge is not merely reinforcing the doctrine of separate spheres, seeing education as a way of preparing women for the private and men for the public sphere; in her fiction of this period the home is seen as central to men as well as women, and both men and women are presented as fulfilling their religious obligations through social service. Education is clearly marked by divisions of gender and class, so that women and men, labourers and professionals, all have their "proper occupations" (177); nevertheless, men like women are seen as more properly directing their attention to the private rather than the public sphere, partly because for Yonge the spiritual and the domestic were often identical. Her critique of education for girls and boys, and for men and women, is based on this criterion. The full title of her novel is The *Daisy Chain or Aspirations: A Family Chronicle*; in it aspirations are properly directed towards the welfare of other people—most immediately those within the family—or towards spiritual goals, not towards public fame and glory.

Both the subject of aspirations and the issue of gender in this novel are explored most fully through the portrait of Ethel May, its central character. She is the most gifted of the May children and has a "great soul and strong nature" (636)—as Sandbach-Dahlstrom shows "she is described in idealizing terms from the very start" (78)—but she is also plain and awkward, and inclined to ignore household tasks and details of her personal appearance for her works of charity or her academic work.[10] The novel shows how Ethel leaves behind this uncertainty about gender identity and accepts her feminine role as a religious duty: the narrative begins when she is fifteen with the afternoon on which her mother is killed and her sister paralysed in a carriage accident; at the same time Ethel sees for the first time the desolate settlement of Cocksmoor, to which she will later dedicate much of her energies. Ethel eventually comes to womanhood through the two channels opened to her on this day, partly through her charitable activities—her brother Harry fraternally describes Ethel as "an odd fish" but adds that "Cocksmoor will make a woman of her" (629)—and partly by taking on the role of her father's housekeeper and companion, and serving as teacher and guardian to her younger brothers and sisters—in fact taking her dead mother's place. It is a measure of the ultimate success of her internalizing of feminine values that she, rather than her more easily and traditionally feminine sisters, takes on the mother's role: while acknowledging her superiority, they are depicted as being jealous of their father's preference for her.

The hard-won femininity of Ethel is especially interesting in relation to education, for she is educated both as a girl and as a boy: she shares with her sisters a traditional feminine education with a prim and elderly governess, aptly named Miss Winter, and gleans a male education (Greek, Latin and mathematics) from her almost equally brilliant elder brother, Norman. In considering gender and education, a comparison between *The Daisy Chain* and *Aurora Leigh* (published the same year; McSweeney xxxvi) is telling both in the strong similarities and the essential differences between the two works. Like Ethel, Aurora has not only a feminine education but also a masculine education, which she regards as an emotional bond to a beloved man as well as an intellectual delight: she learns Greek and Latin from her father, and continues to read his books after he dies. Both these talented girls revel in their classical learning but are very much aware that they are trespassing in male territory. Aurora sees her father's teaching as turning her into an intellectual transvestite: "He wrapt his little daughter in his large / Man's doublet," like the women of Scyros disguising the "young Achilles" in their veils (25; 1.721 28)—a double confusion of genders.[11] Ethel carefully hides all traces of her classical learning away, especially from men, as if it were a kind of immodesty or sexual indecorum: "Ethel would not for the world, that any one should guess at her classical studies—she scarcely liked to believe that even her father knew of them" (7). Some of her family are equally embarrassed at her classical learning; Harry, for instance, "regarded Ethel's attainments as something contraband" (91). Anxiety about the appropriateness of classical learning for women is an undercurrent throughout the novel, and similar anxieties were presumably the basis of Keble's caution to Yonge when she was writing a series of "Conversations on the Catechism" for *The Monthly Packet*: "It occurred to me, whether, when the ladies quote Greek, they have heard their fathers and brothers say things" (Romanes 80). An outright claim to knowledge would be too threatening.

Ethel May and Aurora Leigh are both harassed by the old-fashioned feminine education forced on them, and both narratives present this education in similar terms. Indeed, the lessons Ethel learns from Miss Winter—"What is the latitude and longitude of Otaheite? What are the component parts of brass? Whence is cochineal imported?" (64)— resemble closely those that Aurora learns under her aunt's auspices—"by how many feet / Mount Chimborazo outsoars Teneriffe? / What navigable river joins itself / To Lara" (16; 1.409-12). Similarly they both learn modern languages, drawing, a little mathematics, and sewing. The narrowness and futility of much of the education offered to middle-class young women is made clear in both novel and poem. Both Miss Winter and Aurora's aunt, the providers of a feminine education, are represented as old-fashioned and unduly repressive.[12]

Yet while Aurora dismisses her female education absolutely as disempowering, as teaching the "potential faculty in everything / Of abdicating power in it" (1.441-42), and perceives her poetic vocation as a product of her male education,[13] achieving through it a bond with her dead father, Ethel eventually rejects her male education for the sake of pleasing the father she loves "better than anything else in the world" (434), so as to be "a useful, steady daughter and sister at home" (181) and to continue her demanding charitable activities at Cocksmoor. Unlike Barrett Browning, Yonge represents her intellectual heroine as coming to think of her feminine education as empowering, for Yonge, like Ethel, perceives the home—the parental home—as the locus of power, whereas her masculine classical studies could only lead to the frustration of impotence— as her sister points out she cannot follow her brother to Oxford, or take a first-class degree (181). Her eventual choice leads her into a position of practical and emotional power, establishing her as "the family authority" (The Trial 4).

Until she is compelled to choose, Ethel takes on both forms of education, but under compulsion chooses feminine identity rather than learning, despite her genuine love of the studies that have consoled her in grief and anxiety (DC 43). Her family forces this choice, under the impression that both her health and her femininity are endangered by her studies and by her high ambitions. Miss Winter thinks Ethel will grow up "odd, eccentric, and blue" (179), and her sister Margaret is anxious in case Ethel's "high purposes should run only into romance . . . or grow out into eccentricities and unfeminineness" (60). In forcing Ethel to make her choice she argues, "I don't think dear mamma would have liked Greek and Cocksmoor to swallow up all the little common lady-like things" (182). Ethel's own immediate desire when compelled to choose is to give up her tedious feminine education: "if you would only let me leave off that stupid old French, and horrid dull reading with Miss Winter, I should have plenty of time for everything" (182).[14] Her ultimate decision, however, is that "she must make all give way to papa first, and secondly to Cocksmoor" (183), and accordingly she gives up her Greek studies and keeps on with her charitable activities and her feminine lessons with her governess. Despite her choice, she expresses some resentment at her gender role, though rather indirectly, when she tells the brother with whom she had been studying of this decision: "I was just going to say I hated being a woman, and having these tiresome little trifles—my duty—instead of learning, which is yours, Norman" (182). Norman's unsympathetic response shows that he shares the same concerns about femininity as the rest of the family: "I'm glad you did not . . . for it would have been very silly of you; and I assure you Ethel, it is really time for you to stop, or you would get into a regular learned lady, and be good for nothing. I don't mean that knowing more than other people would make you so, but minding nothing else would" (182). Norman himself, as a promising scholar, is expected to mind nothing else; for Ethel, as a woman, a career as "a regular learned lady" would make her "good for nothing."

The May family, though not without pride in Ethel's abilities, are primarily concerned with her gender identity and her domestic ability. Her father acknowledges Ethel's brilliance but tends to blame any domestic incompetence not on her youth or inexperience but on her studies. When she cannot move the invalid Margaret without causing pain, Dr. May in his anger blames her classical studies: "Ethel will give no attention to anything but her books! I've a great mind to put an end to all the Latin and Greek! She cares for nothing else" (69). He threatens her in the same way when her carelessness nearly causes a serious accident to her little brother: "I'll put a stop to all schools and Greek, if it is to lead to this, and make you good for nothing" (136). Learning Greek is the duty of boys; for girls it may potentially lead to faults of gender that could interfere with the invalid care and child care that are among their duties.

Ethel, the ideal Christian young woman, then, must be educated as a lady to fulfill her domestic responsibilities, and the appropriate place for this is the home. Yonge's position in the contemporary debate about women's education is essentially conservative: although she represents femininity as being compatible with the highest capacity for serious learning, she sees it as incompatible with the single-minded devotion necessary for serious learning. The less focused studies appropriate for women are properly situated not in the new institutions for women's education, which further academic rather than "feminine" learning, but at home. Women's energies are therefore properly dissipated among "all the little common lady-like things" (182).

Yonge's version of a proper feminine education is an education in domestic usefulness and comfort rather than an education in the graces. Although the May girls learn to draw, and some of them learn music, the point of their education is use to others, either in charitable work or in the home. Accomplishments can be seen as having a domestic function in providing family entertainment; certainly Yonge usually shows them in this light rather than presenting them as a sexual lure in the way that, for instance, Eliot presents Rosamond Vincy's accomplishments in *Middlemarch*. Flora May's music entertains the domestic circle, while the Mays' friend Meta Rivers is described by Norman, who is in love with her, as "the perfection of feminine usefulness" (344). The usefulness Norman speaks of lies entirely in her ability to please her wealthy and doting father through her music, her conversation, and her elegant appearance,[15] but in fact Meta makes a point of extending her activities to the practical, using Ethel as a model: she does "plain needlework" for "her poor people" much to Ethel's approval, and learns about "the government of the house," so that the housekeeper comes to her for orders, and she is responsible for paying wages and bills, and so on (344). Even so, Ethel feels that "to be the mistress of a great luxurious house like that does not seem to me the subject of aspirations like Meta's," and she is proved right, for when Meta consents to marry Norman it is clear that she is choosing the prospective missionary as well as the man. As with many of Yonge's women characters, her choices are based on the need for a more active life. Meta, in befriending the Mays and marrying into the family, chooses a life of useful activity rather than one of decorative indolence.

In *The Trial*, which takes up the May family history five years later, again Yonge vindicates a feminine education in domestic usefulness through a comparison of the effects of different modes of teaching, this time by the contrast between the May daughters and Averil Ward, the eldest daughter of a rather pretentious family, a rung down the social ladder from the Mays in having a surgeon rather than a physician as their father. Averil is the product of an institution: she has been educated at an expensive school and turned into a highly accomplished and fashionable young lady. This mode of non-domestic feminine education is obliquely criticized by Averil's failure to cope when her brothers and sisters and both parents become seriously ill with a fever. She infuriates Dr. May by her helplessness: "There sat the girl, dabbling with her water-colours, and her petticoats reaching half across the room, looking like a milliner's doll, and neither she nor her poor mother dreaming of her doing a useful matter" (13), he exclaims. This helpless mode of femininity is placed as inappropriate (and slightly vulgar) by contrast with the useful, nurturing femininity of the May sisters. When poor Averil does try to nurse her family she unnoticingly allows her mother to slip into a fatal coma, and knocks everything in the sickroom down with her huge crinoline and her fashionable hanging sleeves. Meanwhile Ethel May successfully nurses her brother back to health, and Mary May looks after Averil's convalescent little sisters, who show their family's teaching about class and gender in assuming that she cannot be a lady because she provides them with breakfast and lights their nursery fire (16); they have learnt that ladies are useless.

Later, Mary, fatigued by her labours, utters in a dream her "first moral sentiment"—"use before gentility" (23)—but Yonge's implication is clearly that use is in fact identical with gentility, that a true lady is properly concerned not with watercolours and extensive petticoats but with food and warmth, with hearth and home.[16] The merely decorative is vulgar; it is unacceptable on grounds of class as well as of religion. The social ignorance of Averil's parents is suggested by the fact that they provide their daughter with an out-dated "aristocratic" education associating the female with the ornamental, rather than a nineteenth-century middle-class education designed to promote domestic usefulness. Averil represents, therefore, according to Nancy Armstrong's analysis of class and gender, "surface instead of depth, embody[ing] material rather than moral value, and display[ing] idle sensuality instead of constant vigilance and tireless concern for the well-being of others" (Armstrong 20). In fact, the description of Averil's education and its effects is similar in many ways to that of Eliot's Rosamond Vincy, and at the beginning of the novel she functions as the kind of foil to the May sisters that Rosamond provides for Dorothea Brooke and Mary Garth. Only through the experience of the horrors and practical difficulties of life as a settler in Indiana—a near-death experience—does Averil acquire true middle-class womanliness. Her former pretensions are punished by permanent invalidism, but her reformation is rewarded by marriage to a May brother and her domestic function: "her sofa is almost a renewal of the family centre" (365).

Feminine usefulness is not merely confined to the domestic sphere, however; Yonge is by no means just another voice for the angel in the house. The narrative establishes Ethel's superiority as a feminine ideal not only through her central familial role and her father's preference but also through her achievements in "Christianizing" Cocksmoor. In Ethel's moment of decision, when she is forced to choose which of her three educational occupations she will abandon — whether her feminine studies with Miss Winter, her masculine studies with Norman, or her teaching the poor at Cocksmoor — her choice is to abandon her classical education and keep on with her charitable work as well as with her feminine studies. This choice is not presented as an automatic choice of the traditionally feminine woman. Miss Winter, the representative of the old-fashioned concept of the "lady-like," feels that Ethel's energetic work in running the school at Cocksmoor and tending to its pupils is inappropriate for her class, age, and gender; she complains that "those children engross almost all [Ethel's] time and thoughts. She is working [i.e., sewing] for them, preparing lessons, running after them continually. It takes off her whole mind from her proper occupations, unsettles her, and I do think it is beyond what befits a young lady of her age" (177). Miss Winter does not look on Ethel's teaching as her "proper occupation," but Ethel chooses to continue, and the narrative supports her in this — she is successful in her efforts and widely praised for them. Like Miss Winter, Norman is identified as misguided and prejudiced when he expresses distaste for Ethel's work with the dirty, ignorant children. He tells his older sister, Margaret, "I know she has gone crazy after them [the Cocksmoor children] and given up all her Greek for it. It is past endurance!" (209). Margaret's reply ungrammatically supports Ethel in her useful activity rather than in her studies: "it is better they should do what they can for those poor creatures than for Ethel to learn Greek" (209). Later Dr. May in turn refuses to stop Ethel's work for Cocksmoor, despite the toll on her health and that of her sister:

> "I would not take the responsibility of hindering the only pains that have ever been taken with that unlucky place. You don't know that girl Ethel. She began at fifteen, entirely of her own accord, and has never faltered. If any of the children there are saved from perdition, it is owing to her, and I am not going to be the man to stop her." (456)

In regard to Cocksmoor, Ethel is regarded as a saver of souls from perdition. When, for example, at the foundation ceremony for Cocksmoor church the choir sings the words of the psalm, "I will not suffer mine eyes to sleep . . . until I find out a place for the Temple of the Lord" (605), all eyes turn to Ethel (who is carefully established as unconscious of attention and admiration). Near the end of her life, Yonge was to describe the religious motive as the only one that spurred her generation—and Ethel's—to found schools and to teach (*Old Woman's Outlook* 83).

Here, Yonge stresses the religious motive partly in order to distinguish the Mays' involvement in the education of the poor from that of some other contemporary charitable workers. For example, Ethel's religious motivations are carefully differentiated from the reforming ardour of some educationists associated with the early days of feminism. A school like Barbara Leigh Smith's Portman Hall, with its radical programme of mixing genders and classes, avoiding both specifically Christian teaching and learning "by heart," would be anathema to Yonge, especially from a religious point of view. The work of the May family does improve the social condition of Cocksmoor, changing it from "a colony of roughly-built huts of mud, turf, or large blocks of the slate" (23-24) to a village with "the impulse of civilization," despite its persisting "air of poverty" (631). However, their work is essentially directed at bringing the church to Cocksmoor—Ethel's original dream is of a fine church, anonymously funded by her own writing, "with an orderly, religious population, blessing the unknown benefactor, who had caused the news of salvation to be heard among them" (25). The opening of the school shows its Christian basis, as the clergyman

> said a few simple words to the mothers about the wish to teach their children what was right, and to do the best at present practicable; and then told the children that he hoped they would take pains to be good, and mind what they were taught. Then he desired all to kneel down; he said the Collect. (161)

The children's first lessons involve learning the catechism and hearing a bible-reading (162), and Ethel insists that they learn their religious lessons by rote, whether they understand it or not, although she is more adventurous in other subjects, finding a new way of teaching arithmetic, for instance. Yonge establishes that Cocksmoor School is not radical: she carefully avoids associating her fictional social reforms with the reforms of liberalism. Cocksmoor's schoolmistress, Cherry Elwood, is very much the traditional village dame; she does not "fulfill the requirements of modern days" (309), and this limitation is presented largely as a point in her favour, although Ethel can become impatient with her old-fashioned ways:

41

though she taught needlework admirably, and enforced correct reading, and reverent repetition, her strong provincial dialect was a stumbling-block; she could not put questions without book, and nothing would teach her Ethel's rational system of arithmetic. That she was a capital dame, and made the children very good, was allowed; but now and then, when mortified by hearing what was done at Stoneborough, Fordholm, or Abbotstoke, Ethel would make vigorous efforts, which resulted only in her coming home fuming at Cherry's "outrageous dullness." (310)

However, Cherry is religious, and when she is eventually "sent for six months' finish at the Diocesan Training School, while a favourite pupil teacher from Abbotstoke took her place at Cocksmoor" (497), the fear is not that she will come back still ignorant—a strong probability—but that she will be "spoilt" (i.e., made less religious and more self-conscious). The "finishing" process is said to be "much against Ethel's will . . . but we [Mays] thought Cherry not easily spoilt" (508).[17] Ethel may become exasperated with traditional limitations in the energy of her mission to Cocksmoor, but her work there has a solid traditional (Tractarian) basis.

If Cherry is not easily spoilt, no more is Ethel. The narrative establishes a precarious balance; it avoids allowing Ethel an unfeminine and irreligious consciousness of her achievements, while rewarding her fully for her superiority by general public praise and above all by her role as the heart of the family—"no one could get on without her and the Doctor least of all . . . He could not help missing Ethel every minute as the very light of his home" (665). Yonge's rhetoric demands both that Ethel should be rewarded and that she should be unconscious of her own deserts. If ambition is to be acceptable it must not be directed towards the self. It is her "indifference to praise" and "independence of praise" that her mother, shortly before her death, praises in Ethel (49). These qualities are shown in a story-telling game, in which Ethel's story concerns a young king (her own family nickname is "King") who had an old tutor whom he despised for his strictness (Ethel has Miss Winter). He falls in love with Lady Gloria but cannot win her until he is killed in battle. Ethel ends her story thus: "Gloria is given to all who do and suffer truly in a good cause, for faithfulness is glory and that is thine" (287). It turns out that Ethel has altered the original ending to make her hero die, because she thought that "glory could not properly belong to any one here, and if he was once conscious of it would be all spoilt" (287). Ethel in her identification with her hero must lead him to martyrdom, because she feels that sacrifice is the only acceptable form of achievement. It is essentially the sacrificial and self-abnegating nature of her ambitions, foregrounded throughout the novel, that directs readers towards seeing in Ethel the true form of the aspirations of the title page.

V

In *The Daisy Chain* Yonge's narrative also involves the education of boys and men, and on this subject too her Tractarianism leads her both towards an underwriting of the traditional and a critique of those elements in the tradition that are potentially worldly. The old-established institutions connected with male education are criticized directly in this novel, while the new institutions connected with female education are criticized obliquely.

The schools and the university which the May brothers attend are all presented as fostering unhappiness, loss of religious faith, and a decline in moral standards. Richard, the eldest child (eventually an ideal clergyman), who has little academic ability, but is practical, sensible, and affectionate, is said to have been "wretched" in his schooldays (18) and moreover to have been morally affected by the common schoolboy acceptance of cheating: "Richard had been blameless in his whole school course; but though never partaking of the other boys' evil practices . . . his tone had been a little hurt, by sharing the school public opinion of morality" (173-74). He accepts cheating as part of school life, saying that "every one does, and thinks nothing of it . . . we didn't, but most others do, and not bad fellows either" (158). Harry, too, sees school as a place of temptation (95), and his comments finally persuade his father to let him leave school and go to sea. Norman becomes Dux (academic leader of the school and thus in charge of school discipline) but is falsely accused of inciting some boys to vandalism, loses his place as head of the school and a chance of the school scholarship to university, and spends several months in disgrace. Little Tom is soon corrupted by school and "quite ready to accept the feeling prevalent at Stoneborough, that truth was not made for schoolboys" (186). He is also unmercifully bullied. One of his persecutors is expelled (in *The Trial* he murders his uncle and is killed in a Parisian brawl as a suitable punishment), but not before he has induced Tom to drink, swear, and break the Sabbath. When Tom is moved to Eton, Dr. May, an old Stoneborough pupil himself, laments, "I never thought to see the poor old place come to this; but there—when all the better class send their sons to the great public schools, and leave nothing but riff-raff here, one is forced, for a boy's own sake, to do the same" (314). In fact, the only boy who does well at Stoneborough school is Hervey Anderson, who is established as an unprincipled coward.

Yonge evidently shares the prevailing Tractarian view that the middle-class schools were in urgent need of reform and that this reform should be moral reform.[18] Her depiction of life at Stoneborough School suggests that she took considerable interest in the reforms of Tractarian activists like Woodard; in *The Trial* the school is eventually reformed by a new headmaster who had been trained by experience as an under-master "at one of the great schools recently opened for the middle classes" (111)—presumably Hurstpierpoint or Lancing. He is appalled at how Stoneborough has declined morally and academically: "the whole tone of the school had degenerated . . . scholarship was at a low ebb" (111). He improves the school gradually but so successfully that the little May grandson from New Zealand is eventually sent to Stoneborough school. Yonge's interest in boys' school reform is also briefly touched on in the novel which follows *The Daisy Chain, Dynevor Terrace*, which involves the attempted reform of a slightly less prestigious local grammar school. Its new Tractarian master speaks of his employment as an opportunity to reach "the important middle-class, whom I would do anything to train in sound principles" (235).

Although Oxford was the springboard of Tractarianism, "the Oxford Movement," the university shares in Yonge's distrust for educational institutions. In the Oxford scenes in *The Daisy Chain*, according to Romanes, "some hints are given of the stress and strain which so many of the best of Oxford felt in these years after the [1845] disappearance of Newman [into the outer darkness of Roman Catholicism]" (73). When he goes up to Oxford on a Balliol scholarship, Norman, as a brilliant debater and a supporter of "Church principles," is compelled into constant discussions about his beliefs, which temporarily arouse in him religious doubts and a sense that he is blinded by his own rhetoric, seeing reality in a "magic mirror." Meta responds with alarm, "I thought old Oxford was the great guardian nurse of truth! I am sure she cannot deal in magic mirrors or such frightful things" (429). Dr. May is even more aghast at the prospect of Norman's loss of faith and partly blames his spiritual danger on his education: "he seemed somewhat inclined to hold poor Oxford in horror" (521). Altogether, although Yonge never analytically criticizes the male educational institutions, her narrative directly presents them as places of constant moral, psychological, spiritual, and —for poor little Tom—physical danger.

Yet despite her imaginings of the harm done in various ways by and to boys in large groups, she voiced and would continue to voice the conventional opinion that boys and girls differ in the way they behave in groups.[19] She told Emily Davies, the founder of Girton, of her own "decided objections to bringing large masses of girls together" (Battiscombe, *Yonge* 146) and later voiced her belief that "the feminine nature is not one to improve by being massed together" (*Womankind* 27). Yonge's rationale is based on the feminine domestic role; she argues that "girls . . . certainly deteriorate in proportion as the sense of family life is lost," while on the other hand "most boys are improved by free intercourse with their own kind in large numbers" (*Womankind* 31).[20] While insisting on the traditional gender distinction that allows boys to prepare for a public life and girls for a private life, she describes a world in which that distinction is baseless, and in operation actually works in favour of girls (and the private) rather than boys (and the public).[21] Her fictions consistently suggest that men and women alike "deteriorate . . . as the sense of family life is lost."

The dangers of schools and universities as Yonge presents them are partly related to the competitive spirit that is fostered in them as a basic part of their structure. The boys are constantly ranked, and their future depends on their comparative standing: "all schoolboys," as Mrs. May notes, live "a life of emulation" (49). When Norman wins the highest position in the school, his family, despite its doctrinal beliefs about worldly ambition, is exalted and Norman's schoolfellows dejected. Harry gloats, "You should have seen how Anderson grinned—he is only fourth—down below Forder, and Cheviot, and Ashe," and Ethel responds, "Well I did not think Norman would have been before Forder and Cheviot. That is grand" (104). Norman's achievements, unlike Ethel's, are a matter of family honour; they are displayed rather than concealed. When Norman returns to school after an illness, "everyone was just now anxiously watching Norman, especially his father who strove in vain to keep back all manifestations of his earnest desire to see him retain his post" (174). Norman shares his family's competitive spirit in relation to his academic work, boasting to Ethel that he has never been beaten "by any one, except by you, when you take pains" (22).

Yet although Norman's academic ambitions are regarded as creditable by his family, as Ethel's never could be,[22] he, like Ethel, has to turn his aspirations away from personal fulfillment and towards practical usefulness. Eventually he decides to leave the "feverish life of competition and controversy" (517) that he finds in Oxford, and to dedicate himself as a missionary to New Zealand and to a life of practical use, like his sister's. So both brother and sister make the choice of abandoning classical studies and taking up a life of service, a life which Yonge regards not just as more appropriate to a woman but as more appropriate to a Christian. Initially Norman feels that Ethel's work at Cocksmoor is unworthy of her:

"Let those who are fit for nothing else go and drone over A, B, C, with ragged children if they like. It is just their vocation . . . minds of a superior kind are intended for higher purposes, not to be wasted in this manner" (209). Eventually, without losing his disdain for the less fortunate or his sense of repulsion at dirt, ignorance, and unfamiliar manners, he comes to accept social service as his duty, fired by the example of a learned but humble old clergyman. Reflecting on his own academic distinctions he says, "I see now that these things that puff us up, and seem the whole world to us now all end in nothing but such as this! Think of old Mr. Wilmot, once carrying all before him, but deeming all his powers well bestowed in fifty years teaching of clowns!" (352). Norman hardly achieves a state of humility or even ordinary human fellow-feeling with "clowns"—ordinary working people; he does, however, come to feel that competition is as destructive to the winners as to the losers.

Yonge firmly establishes competition as morally deleterious and foregrounds the competitive nature of all interactions at school and university but, perhaps out of respect for tradition, never explicitly criticizes the practices that she shows to be so harmful. Her narrative does establish that for men as well as for women the public sphere and public praise are dangerous. Domestic obscurity is the proper choice for both sexes, for Norman as well as Ethel, for Dr. May as well as for his wife. Norman chooses obscurity rather than possible fame, and so does his father. After meeting an old friend from medical school, Sir Matthew Fleet, now a distinguished London specialist, Dr. May speaks of his sorrow at seeing his friend's development into "a mere machine with a moving spring of self-interest," and he thinks with gratitude of the family home in Stoneborough and of the early marriage which kept him from ending up like Sir Matthew: "I never knew fully till now the blessing it was that your dear mother was willing to take me so early, and that this place was open to me with all its home connexions and interests. I am glad I never had anything to do with London" (130). Domestic values counterbalance and finally outweigh competitiveness, and thus he urges on Norman the lesson he will eventually take to himself: "Take care the love of rising and pushing never gets hold of you; there's nothing that faster changes a man from his better self" (130). Dr. May is essentially the domestic male, and even professionally his success comes from his nurturing qualities; his tender care for his patients is reiterated throughout the novel.

The Trial replays the version of masculinity thus displayed in *The Daisy Chain.* Young Tom May, a protégé of Sir Matthew Fleet who is naturally both able and ambitious, eventually leaves behind his worldly goals of success and prestige in London, and takes over his father's provincial practice. This transformation comes about largely through his love for Averil Ward; because she is in poor health and has a lower social standing, he learns both sympathy for weakness, and tolerance for social differences. Ethel rejoices that "the least unselfish nature has from first to last done the most unselfish things. No one of us has ever given up so much as Tom, and I am sure he will be happy in it" (365). Tom's narrative is the essential Yonge narrative of "giving up," but significantly it is giving up the public for the private and the domestic. Tom, like Norman, must follow Ethel's example, and learn to value not public but private rewards.

Much of the work of the Victorian educational reformers seems to imply that ideally girls' education should be more like that of boys. Yonge certainly never suggests that boys' education should be like that of girls, but she does imply that male standards should be more like those associated with the female. *The Daisy Chain* suggests that one of the functions of education is to reinforce gender roles, so that girls learn their feminine role of submission and self-abnegation while boys learn through competition. Yonge thus confirms the importance of gender distinctions, yet she eschews a domestic double standard, for the values that she associates with male education are finally condemned, and feminine values are virtually identified with Christian values. Use and domesticity are finally placed above both prestige and success.

CHAPTER TWO

"Something to Do":
The Clever Woman of the Family (1865)
and the Question of Women's Work

"Here am I, able and willing, only longing to task myself to the uttermost, yet tethered down to the merest mockery of usefulness by conventionalities" (3). The woman who speaks for so many of her prosperous and frustrated sisters is not, as one might suppose, Florence Nightingale in the fury of her wasted youth, but Rachel Curtis, the central character of *The Clever Woman of the Family* (1865), Yonge's contribution to the lively contemporary debate on women and work. This novel, like *The Daisy Chain*, celebrates the domestic and religious lives of women; but it also explores and vindicates a fierce and frustrated yearning for useful work that is quite unlike Ethel's sense of her vocation both at home and at Cocksmoor. It is a conservative novel centred on a vigorous, unconventional, and independent woman, and many of Yonge's novels can be described in these terms. This aspect of her fiction arose perhaps from the double compulsion under which she lived. As noted in the Introduction, Yonge needed urgently both the approval of her conservative father and the freedom to write. She acknowledged frankly her need for paternal approval (Romanes 16), and the strength of her drive to fiction was a large element in her success. Her capacity to inspire in her readers what A. S. Byatt calls "narrative greed" (335) is the counterpart of her own lifelong appetite to tell stories: "Oh, I must have written" (Coleridge 153), Yonge exclaimed when asked about her career. Yet Yonge's treatment of women and work is not merely an expression of her personal position as a daughter and a writer. Like her treatment of women's education, it is an aspect of her Tractarianism and corresponds in many ways with the thought and action of other women and men in the Oxford Movement.

It is also a part of an urgent contemporary debate. The women's movement itself was more focused than it had ever been before: the reforms in women's education were launched and the question of work for the middle-class woman had taken on a new importance. In *The Clever Woman in the Family* Yonge places herself far more deliberately than she had done in any of her previous work in the context of an on-going discussion on women's issues, slyly pointing at various foibles in the contemporary women's movement and openly responding to their claims. *The Daisy Chain* enters the contemporary debate about women's education without acknowledging it; *The Clever Women of the Family*, however, confronts the current debate about women and work with quiet satire.

The Tractarians, despite their principled traditionalism and hostility to all causes associated with liberalism, took the question of women's work very seriously, largely because of their belief in the spiritual importance of good works as well as faith. For women like Yonge and Christina Rossetti, who wanted to dedicate their energies, Anglo-Catholicism was by no means merely restrictive; it provided a kind of consecration of their labours. It was potentially liberating, too, for women with very different kinds of abilities. The establishment of Anglican sisterhoods from 1845 onwards, through the endeavours of dedicated Tractarians, enabled the church more effectively to educate, nurse, and generally help the poor and also provided certain women with a channel for their energies, by broadening their existing narrow range of possibilities. Perhaps an even more important function of the sisterhoods was to demonstrate the church's support for women's claim to effectiveness and responsibility. The Tractarian movement played a complex part in that shifting of middle-class ideology of which Mary Poovey writes "because it was always in the making, it was always open to revision, dispute and the emergence of oppositional formations" (3).

This chapter begins by indicating the importance of the question of women's work in the mid-Victorian period and discussing the Tractarian position on this matter, along with the growth of the Anglican sisterhoods. It then explores Yonge's own treatment of women's work and women's capacities, both through the situations and characters she invents and through the structure of her plots, focusing especially on *The Clever Woman of the Family*, which dates from the period of most intense concern with questions of women's employment. This novel's contemporaneity is presumably what Yonge's friend and biographer, Christabel Coleridge, objected to as "a controversial element, which . . . detracts from its charm" (Coleridge 230). Public discussion of women's role compelled Yonge in this novel, which is primarily concerned with work and women, to articulate her position about gender roles. One result of this obligatory explicitness is a somewhat uneasy tone in Yonge's treatment of the feminine in this novel. Nevertheless, despite her ingrained distaste for the blatantly emancipated woman, and the conservative "stayat-home" propaganda of such early novels as *The Daisy Chain* (Vicinus 11), Yonge provided her countless young readers with models of able, energetic and achieving women, and created a recognizable version of her society in which such achievements could be viewed as an acceptable part of the life of a good and religious woman. Her female characters have interesting alternatives to marriage, while in her plots she carefully avoids treating marriage as the inevitable resolution.

I

"Something to do was her cry" (7) writes Charlotte Yonge of Rachel Curtis, who longs to fight against the "one mass of misery and evil" (3) which crushed the Victorian poor. Rachel's cry sounds very familiar to readers of mid-nineteenth-century texts: "from every rank and every class of women there rises up the cry that work is wanted and that no work is to be had," remarked J. Boyd-Kinnear in 1869 (Hollis 54). At about the same time, Dinah Mulock Craik commented on the various remedies to this problem, "possible and impossible, from compulsory wifehood in Australia to voluntary watch-making at home," which were promulgated incessantly in "book, pamphlet, newspaper, and review" (80). For some women the need for work was purely economic, but other, wealthier women also needed to assuage their dread that their lives might be wasted.

Yonge's language—the opposition between "something to do" and "nothing to do"—is part of the discourse of women's work at mid-century. In *Cassandra* (1852) Florence Nightingale, writing from bitter personal experience, expresses the plight of prosperous middle-class women in one simple five-word paragraph:

> They have nothing to do. (36)

Anna Jameson uses the same words when writing of

> women who, in the midst of all the splendor of a luxurious home, have perished by a slow wasting disease of body and of mind, because they had nothing to do—no sphere of activity commensurate with the large mental powers or passionate energy of character with which God had endowed them. (117)

Charlotte Brontë's Caroline Helstone and Shirley Keeldar (in *Shirley*, 1849) share the same desire for useful occupation:

> "Caroline," demanded Miss Keeldar, abruptly, "don't you wish you had a profession—a trade?"

"I wish it fifty times a-day. As it is, I often wonder what I came into the world for. I long to have something absorbing and compulsory to fill my head and my hands and occupy my thoughts" (235)

Emily Davies, the founder of Girton College, Cambridge, states bluntly her belief in the primary importance of this question: "in considering the various means by which the present condition of women may be improved the most obvious is that of extending the range of occupations open to them" (6). The Recorder of Hull in the mid-1860s voiced a general perception when he declared that "human ingenuity could hardly more admirably occupy itself, than in discovering and devising new and creditable modes of occupation for females, especially the younger ones, of the middle classes" (Davies 1). Martha Vicinus argues convincingly that, despite the increase in absolute numbers of unmarried women, the problem was one of perception rather than of reality (27). Nevertheless, whatever its basis the most important problem associated with the "woman question" at this period was clearly that of women and work. At a time when work was regarded not as the curse of Adam but as a Christian privilege for all people—"after Christ, work turns to privilege," claims Barrett Browning's Romney Leigh (*Aurora Leigh* 280; 8.450)—naturally unemployment or underemployment in any social group would have been more readily noted and more strongly deplored.[1]

This perceived problem gave a focus to feminist activity and discussion in the 1850s and 1860s; the pressure to improve women's educational opportunities, discussed in the last chapter, continued and eventually intensified, but the new focus was on the issue of work. Accordingly, women and sympathetic men in several parts of England organized employment societies and started up training schemes and employment registers. The *English Woman's Journal* (started in 1858) began an employment register, and in 1859 its founders, including Bessie Parkes, Barbara Leigh Smith, and Jessie Boucherett—"the Langham Place group"—formed the Society for Promoting the Employment of Women (SPEW), which aimed at opening up suitable fields of employment to middle-class women (Burstyn 127; Herstein 125-48). They soon began to help small groups train for and find employment in such fields as hairdressing, photography, book-keeping, administration of charities, engraving, proof-reading, and so on. After the founding of the Charity Organization Society in 1869, women were trained as rent collectors, district visitors and sanitary inspectors (Hollis 202). SPEW ran the printing business which under Emily Faithfull printed *The English Woman's*

Journal, using women as compositors. Similar societies were organized in the provinces. In 1860 in Newcastle-upon-Tyne a public meeting carried the resolution "that a committee be formed in aid of the Society for promoting the employment of women . . . to receive subscriptions, gather and diffuse information, and to encourage by personal influence, the introduction of women into such occupations as are suitable to their powers" (Davies 28). Durham had a similar committee (Herstein 143). Meanwhile another possible solution to the problem of women and work was initiated through the foundation of the Female Middle Class Emigration Society (Herstein 143). The variety of initiatives outlined here indicates that, at least until in the mid-1860s, when the proposed reform bill that was to become the Reform Act of 1867 focused attention on the pressing political and legal issues relating to the status of women, the active centre of feminist activity in Britain was the search for new modes of employment.

II

Most of the women involved in the new ventures, of course, held very different views on church, family, and society from Yonge's, but they were nevertheless working towards a similar goal: Josephine Butler deplores young women's "temptation to frivolity, the absence of all mental resource, emptyheadedness, love of dress" (Butler xx) as morally destructive, just as Yonge does.[2] Yonge and other Tractarians disliked the conventional, limited view of the middle-class woman as much as the feminists did. They deplored the worldliness of the generally accepted belief that a lady "must not work for profit" and that "if a woman is obliged to work, at once she (although she may be Christian and well bred) loses that peculiar position which the word *lady* conventionally designates" (Holcombe 4). Yonge suggests in *Womankind* (35) that in fact receiving pay conferred a special sense of "earnestness and consistency," and throughout her fiction she writes of women's longing for hard work. While the Tractarians believed strongly in obligations to the family, they saw spiritual deprivation and danger (in the words of Yonge's magazine, *The Monthly Packet*, in 1868) in the fate of "these Christian gentlewomen who . . . are living in the world of London, hedged round by conventionalities, trammeled by the usages and unable from some hindering cause or another, to 'come out' and live a life entirely apart from the world, which is (whether we like to recognize the fact or not) at war with God" (Allchin 116).

The Tractarians' concern with the problem of middle-class woman and work follows inevitably from their theological position, for unlike the Evangelicals, they believed that salvation depended not on faith alone, but on good works, as well. They believed, that is, that all Christians are obliged to use to the full their talents and energies in the service of God and that such works have a sanctifying effect, the deeds augmenting faith and holiness in the doer. Yonge's own distinction between Tractarianism and Evangelicalism emphasizes this point. She contrasts the Evangelical who "lays stress on the individual sense of pardon through faith in the Atonement, and the Catholic, which builds on that faith the belief in the power of the Sacraments, and of *personal holiness and meritorious action through the aid of the Holy Spirit*" (*Womankind* 214—my emphasis). Isaac Williams, like Yonge a devoted pupil of John Keble who shared Keble's concern with "meritorious action," writes in Tract 87 (1840), "On Reserve" (which aroused a storm of disapproval), that

> charitable works alone will make man charitable, and the more anyone does charitable works the more charitable he will become; that is to say the more will he love his neighbour and love God; for a charitable work is a work that proceeds from charity or the love of God, and which only can be done by the good Spirit of God. (Jay 120-21)

In her novels Yonge foregrounds the spiritual effectiveness of good works—in the development of Ethel May, for instance—and also comments rather sharply on the hostility of the Evangelicals to the notion of salvation through work as well as faith. In *The Three Brides* (1876) Bessie Duncombe, having tirelessly and heroically nursed the victims of a fever epidemic, is warned by her strict Evangelical mother-in-law against "thinking there is any merit in works of mercy" (313). Yonge's heroines and heroes, as good Tractarians, are much given to "doing" good works —though to the Evangelicals "doing ends in death" (*Pillars* 2.277). When Averil Ward in *The Trial* says to her brother, Leonard, "men do, and women suffer," Leonard comments aptly, "that's trite!" and continues, "I like you to *do*—as you call it—Miss May *does*, and everyone that is worth anything" (71)—Miss May being of course the redoubtable Ethel.[3] I do not mean to suggest that the Evangelical movement was less active in charitable endeavours; that would be ridiculous in view of the work of such famous evangelicals as Lord Shaftesbury. However, because the Tractarians believed in the spiritual efficacy of works, they necessarily believed that women as well as men should have abundant opportunity for good works so that they could dedicate their lives and their energies to the glory of God and thus gain in faith and holiness. For instance, the membership of such a devoted Tractarian as Christina Rossetti in the "Portfolio Club," a group of women artists started by the feminists Bessie Rayner Parkes and Barbara Leigh Smith in the 1850s to allow women artists to share their writing and their sketches (Leighton 123), shows how acceptable Tractarian women found the expression of a serious sense of vocation. For these reasons the Tractarians were the first and most active workers in the movement to establish working sisterhoods, although as Vicinus shows, the Evangelicals were to follow their example (46-50).

III

The new Anglican sisterhoods grew rapidly throughout most of Charlotte Yonge's adult life—according to A. M. Allchin, from eighty-six sisters in 1861 to between two and three thousand by the end of the century (201). The religious communities for women started far earlier than those for men and grew far faster (Ollard 173), presumably because they answered more specific needs. They were a valuable token of Anglican support for women's effectiveness and their spirituality at a time when it was acceptable to deny publicly the possibility of women doing any useful task outside their homes. As early as 1839, Edward Pusey wrote of the desirability of sisterhoods within the Anglican church, acknowledging women's urgent need to work usefully:

> I want very much to have one or more societies of *Soeurs de la Charité* formed: I think them desirable 1) in themselves as belonging to and fostering a high tone in the Church, 2) as giving a holy employment to many who yearn for something, 3) as directing zeal which will otherwise go off in some irregular way or go over to Rome. (Anson 222)

Pusey acted on his own beliefs: he was associated with the foundation of several of the sisterhoods which sprang up across England, and he continued to stress publicly the need for the church to use women's work and women's longing for self-dedication. At an 1862 Church Congress in Oxford, for instance, he repeated that "the longing for the religious life is deeply and widely spread among our Christian ladies" (Allchin 141), and the growth of the sisterhoods proved him right for some years to come.

Even as Pusey spoke, several small sisterhoods already existed. In June, 1841, Marian Rebecca Hughes, who was later to found and to become Mother Superior of the Communion of the Holy and Undivided Trinity in Oxford, had taken her vows, and in the summer of 1844 Miss Moore had moved into John Keble's parish in order to place herself under his spiritual direction and lead "an ordered life of prayer, churchgoing, and

54

good works" (Ollard 170-71). In 1845 the first actual sisterhood was set up, and several others rapidly followed. Their charitable activities were extensive; the Tractarian emphasis on education was reflected in their various teaching activities, but they were also involved in nursing and in helping prostitutes. The sisterhoods were evidently institutions where any appetite for hard work could be glutted, and just as Yonge's novels foreground women's appetite for meaningful work, so did the sister-hoods; all the early orders were active rather than contemplative.[4] The Wantage sisterhood (of which Yonge was to become in 1868 an exterior sister) organized a range of educational activities, including a school for pupil teachers, a boarding school for young ladies, and a hostel for women "home students" in Oxford. Sisters of various communities be-came well-known as nurses; some of them went to Scutari in 1854 with Florence Nightingale, who viewed their efforts with mixed feelings. They were especially useful in the epidemics which were so frequent and devastating a feature of Victorian summers—the Sisters of the Poor nursed the victims of the cholera epidemic in London in 1866 and of the smallpox outbreaks in 1870 and 1871 (Anson 400), while the St. John's Nursing Sisterhood helped in an epidemic of typhoid fever in the Staf-fordshire Colliery district (Anson 282). The sisterhoods also ran hostels for women leaving prison, for young offenders, and for women inebriates (Anson 254). According to Jameson, however, "what has been consid-ered as the particular province of all Sisters of Charity deserving the name" was "the management of Penitentiaries and Houses of Refuge for the erring and the fallen of their own sex" (79), such as the House of Charity in Highgate, run by the Sisterhood of All Saints, of which Chris-tina Rossetti was an associate member.

Despite the crude hostilities of *Punch*, the delight of the press in the scandals and riots that marked the early history of the women's commu-nities, and a predictable mixture of public mockery and mistrust,[5] the new sisterhoods were accepted in some non-Tractarian quarters with a surprising degree of tolerance. No doubt one reason why parts of the Victorian general public found them less threatening than might have been expected was that one essential quality of a sister of charity is self-abnegation, a quality comfortably identifiable with womanhood. These women could be useful, hard-working, and dedicated to their work without "losing their femininity"—that is, without calling too far into question conventional concepts of gender or threatening the status quo. Many people besides Tractarians, however, positively welcomed the sis-terhoods usually for the simple reason that they were perceived as helping solve two of the most notorious problems of Victorian England, the enormous social needs of the poor and the yearning of many middle-class women for a vocation. As Pauline Nestor says,

> The most convincing defence of sisterhoods, before which even the most skeptical seemed to bow, was an appeal to their efficacy as agents of practical philanthropy. Anna Jameson, Barbara Bodichon, Frances Cobbe, and Florence Nightingale all gave voice to the belief that the drift of so many women into the Catholic Church was due to the fact that Catholicism offered them the opportunity to "throw their energies into a sphere of definite utility."
>
> (19)

These last few words are quoted from Jameson's book *Sisters of Charity*, a long discourse on the desirability of active (not contemplative) orders outside the Roman Catholic communion: "I am no friend to nunneries," she claims (and disposes quickly of the life of prayer), "but it is very different with the active orders and I should certainly like to see amongst us some institutions which if not exactly like them, should supply their place" (70-71). This wish is based on her perception of the urgent need of middle-class women for serious work. In the same vein, Dinah Mulock Craik believed that in many women the need for real work was so urgent that it could lead to "confirmed invalidism or hypochondria or actual insanity" and, despite mixed feelings, honoured the sisterhoods accordingly (54). Barbara Leigh Smith Bodichon, without quite evoking madness (or death, as Jameson does), believed that "happier by far is a Sister of Charity or Mercy than a young lady at home without a work or a lover" (Auerbach 195). Florence Nightingale wrote of sisterhoods: "each was employed according to . . . her vocation; there was work for all; but there is no such possibility in the family."[6] Male painters may have taken the erotic and (to the male ego) flattering view of the nun as a beautiful woman retreating from an unhappy love affair (Casteras 157-84); for the women most deeply concerned with the subject, however, the sisterhoods were welcome because they offered women a sphere of hard, useful, serious work. Victorian feminists perceived the practical contribution the Tractarians made through the religious orders to the advancement of women.[7]

Effective though they were, the sisterhoods, in fact, involved few of the large numbers of unmarried middle-class women. Their significance perhaps lies less in their provision of a possible alternative career than in the church's acceptance of women's capacity to devote their lives and energies to work outside the family. Dean Church, the historian of the Oxford Movement, spoke strongly on this subject when he preached on "the Ministry of Women" at the Annual Festival of the sisterhood at Wantage in 1875:

> Here the plan of a life of labour for women—intelligent, beneficent, fervent labour for Christ—labour serious, habitual, sustained, like the labour of men, broke through the spell which condemned it as unnatural and unprecedented, and became a reality. . . . On this anniversary, we have a right, we have cause, to bless God, that the ministry of women has again become one of the recognized institutions of the English Church.   (Allchin 94)

In accepting such sisterhoods the church accepted that serious work for women was not "unnatural"; if it was "unprecedented," the early sisters created a precedent—an important precedent. The sisterhoods gave women the opportunity of demonstrating their organizational abilities and their ability to fill responsible positions in the institutions which they founded, as well as their ability to work together in groups without male intervention.

However, the aims of the sisterhoods and their supporters were a world away from later concepts of the virtues of self-direction and self-fulfillment. They were working in and partly dependent on a conspicuously male-dominated hierarchy. Moreover, a woman's duty to her family was still primary; the conventional view was that only when there were no significant family duties could a woman seriously consider a sisterhood. Much of the adverse publicity concerning the sisterhoods arose from family opposition—claims of a superior right to the services of a daughter or a sister.[8] Bishop Tait, an opponent of Tractarianism, voiced the accepted view in 1865:

> I do fully approve of ladies who have no home duties and who think they are fitted for such work associating themselves together for the care of the poor and the sick—I believe no blessing will ever come on work, however self-denying, which is undertaken to the neglect of those higher duties which belong to home life and which are imposed directly by God Himself.
>
> (Anson 303)

As John Shelton Reed points out in an important article on the subject, joining a sisterhood could be part of a rebellion against parental authority (233). Yet on the whole, because the clergymen who had a powerful influential role were likely to discourage the vocation of any woman with existing "higher duties belonging to home life," the sisterhoods were an uncertain alternative to a woman who found her family duties irksome, or who didn't see them as duties at all, or who longed for escape from an abusive or distasteful home. They could certainly be imagined as allowing for self-devotion, but although Anthony Harrison's view of them as "radically liberating for the women who became involved with them" (98) has considerable justification, the road to liberation was at the best precarious.[9]

IV

Yonge's emphasis in her fiction on the useful activity of women should be understood in the context of the rather unexpected and unintentional contribution by Tractarians to the Women's Movement. Certainly she repeatedly creates women who are competent or excellent workers, in their homes, in sisterhoods and in the outside world—and increasingly, after about 1870, paid workers; in novel after novel she writes of women's hunger for work.[10] She worked *pro Ecclesia Dei*—for the Church of God— and expected others to do likewise. She foregrounds the need for work but like her fellow-Tractarians describes it not in terms of self-fulfillment but in terms of fulfillment of one's duty to God. Arguably she rationalized her own compulsion to write by interpreting her writing—her chosen work—in this way.

Her fullest fictional discussion of the concept of the church as directing women's work comes in *The Pillars of the House* (2.362-63), when she describes two elaborate cartoons, versions of Raphael's *School of Athens*. One depicts women at work outside the church, showing that "something of vanity and vexation of spirit pervaded all," while the other shows women at work under the aegis of the church, to express the artist's belief that

> while woman works merely for the sake of self-cultivation, the clever grow conceited and emulous, the practical harsh and rigid, the light or dull vain, frivolous, deceitful by way of escape, and it all gets absurd. But the being handmaids of the Church brings all right; and the School of St. Sophia develops even the intellect.

Geraldine Underwood, the artist, is evidently her author's mouthpiece here. In *Womankind* (1876), a rather depressing non-fiction work of the same period, Yonge directly expresses a similar belief:

> Let her feel herself responsible to the one great Society [i.e., the church] of which she is a part, and let her look for the services that she can fulfil by head or hands, by superintendence or by labour, by pen or pencil, by needle or by activity, by voice or by music, by teaching or by nursing—nay, by the gentle sympathy and earnest prayers of an invalid; and the vague discontent is appeased. (7)

58

She continues even more emphatically: "it is only as a daughter of the Church that woman can have her place or be satisfied as to her vocation" (8). Work is thus a matter of duty or necessity rather than a matter of self-fulfillment—or rather one can be fulfilled through only doing one's duty. Her beliefs apply to both genders: Lance Underwood responds to his sister's cartoons with the comment, "it might as well be man as woman" (*Pillars* 2.363), and indeed Yonge portrays Lance as a gifted and sensitive man who sacrifices his musical genius to his family's needs and to his own conception of his duty—an almost womanly deed (Lance's self-abnegation is discussed more fully in my conclusion, below). On the whole, however, Yonge naturally is far more interested in the way women approach their life and work, and thus deals more closely with woman's work "for the Church of God."

A. M. Allchin indicates accurately both the limits and the extent of Yonge's beliefs about women and work: "At no time has she any use for women who set themselves up in competition with men. But on the other hand she urges to the full the rights and duties of women in their own particular sphere" (118-19). Eventually Yonge comes to define that sphere fairly generously. Her notion of women's sphere finally includes the arts and sciences, business, education, and many other fields: the jobs she lists as acceptable in *Womankind* include those of hospital nurse, nursery nurse, telegraph clerk, dressmaker, teacher, as well as employment in music, literature, and the visual arts (236-39). About the only profession that she consistently perceives as unsuitable for a woman was medicine: "except for certain kinds of practice, and for superior nursing, it does not seem as if enough would be gained to make it desirable to outrage feminine instincts—and those of men, by the full course of scientific training" (*Womankind* 105).[11] Accordingly, she portrays her sole woman doctor (Janet Brownlow in *Magnum Bonum*, 1879) as offending against gender: not only is she imperceptive, incompetent and unscrupulous, she is also ill-dressed, socially inept, and plain. Apart from this interesting exception, however, Yonge acknowledges the variety of possible fields open to women.[12]

Perhaps the most significant quality of Yonge's treatment of women and work is its centrality in many of her novels. She is unusual among Victorian novelists, even among Victorian women novelists, in actually stressing and demonstrating the important role of work in the lives of her female characters.[13] Although Maggie Tulliver becomes a governess, her professional life is "off-stage"; the action of *The Mill on the Floss* deals with her relations with Tom, Philip, and Stephen. Jane Eyre's teaching career is more central, but what matters to the novel is not Jane as a teacher but

Jane's relation to herself and to Rochester and St. John Rivers. The point is that while Jane's work leads her to human relationships, the work of Cherry Underwood and Ethel May leads them to God: and one advantage of God over man as a goal is that he is not likely to ask one to abandon one's serious pursuits to care for him, as after all one's serious pursuits can conveniently be interpreted as caring for him. And statistically he is far less likely to distract one from one's serious pursuits by pregnancy. Yonge never presents a woman as frustrated because she is not married; she is far more likely to express the frustrations of being without appropriate work. Indeed, she comments on the inadequacy of the marriage novel through Ethel May, who watches her father with an old friend and thinks "how insufficient are those pictures of life that close with the fever-dream of youthful passion, and leave untold those years of the real burthen of manhood, and still more the tranquil brightness when toil has been over-lived, and the setting sun gilds the clouds that are drifting away" (*The Trial* 280). Carolyn Heilbrun has argued that "women writers (and women politicians, academics, psychoanalysts) have been unable to imagine for other women, fictional or real, the self they have in fact achieved" (72).[14] Yonge is one woman writer to whom this does not apply, both because of the strength of her religious convictions and because of her experience of the urgent need to write. Christina Rossetti, Yonge's co-religionist, is another such, perhaps because "renunciation of the world, with all its misguided social institutions and material temptations, is the unique route to self-fulfillment" for Rossetti, as Anthony Harrison argues (97), demonstrating the implicit attacks on marriage in her work.

As editor as well as novelist, Yonge refused to treat love as pivotal. She turned down submissions to *The Monthly Packet* on these grounds: "I am sorry to say 'Aylton' will not do," she replies to one writer, explaining that "the whole turns exclusively on love, and though that is not a subject that I at all wish to omit from the Monthly Packet I would rather have it as an accessory and not a principle" (Battiscombe, *Yonge* 113). The young Mrs. Humphry Ward, while still the less formidable Miss Mary Arnold, received a rejection on similar grounds: "I do not go on the principle of no love at all, and letting nobody marry, but I do not think it will do to have it the whole subject and interest of the story," Yonge explains (Sutherland, *Ward* 38). For Yonge, whose novels are strongly gendered but curiously asexual, the ultimate fulfillment of a women's destiny is not marriage but salvation; the ultimate pleasure is not sex but work. Judith Rowbotham writes of Yonge as indicating that "marriage leading to motherhood was the most desirable and productive end for the majority of readers to imitate" (29), but in fact she presents a striking number of happy, productive, unmarried women.

Her stated beliefs never changed. She continued throughout her career to praise family life. Yet increasingly often she creates female characters who choose other kinds of fulfillment and describes more fully the urges that compel women to work. Women's drive to work and the necessity to use this drive is one of her repeated motifs. Ethel May is a case in point, for she has "such a spirit of energy in her that if she does not act, she will either speculate and theorize, or pine and prey on herself" (*DC* 151), while Albinia Kendal in *The Young Stepmother* takes on a depressive husband with three difficult adolescent children partly because she wants to use up her surplus energies. Yonge's energetic women also work professionally. This is especially true of many of the novels that follow *The Clever Woman of the Family*, her own pointed contribution to the contemporary debate on middle-class women and work. While Yonge does not explicitly acknowledge in this novel the contemporary ferment about the employment of women, any reader in 1865 would have recognized the context in which it was written. Her central character, Rachel Curtis, devotes all her energies to women's work—her own need for work, the suitable employment of local poor women, and establishing an organization and a journal that concern women's work. Rachel's activities and ambitions provide a kind of travesty of the actual achievements of the London feminists of the period.

V

The Clever Woman of the Family is Charlotte Yonge's *Emma*.[15] Rachel Curtis is, like Emma Woodhouse, the brightest and most energetic person in her immediate domestic and social circle, the child of a fussy, kind and rather dim invalid parent with a similarly pleasantly dim elder sister. She is also an heiress and a member of the most influential local family. Like Emma, Rachel is both frustrated and made overconfident (and therefore gullible) by her position both in her family and in local society. She makes embarrassing blunders, just as Emma does, about other people, preaching heroism to Alexander Keith through the example of an unnamed hero who turns out to be Alexander himself—and offering to help Ermine Williams prepare her writings for the press, not knowing that Ermine is a distinguished though pseudonymous essayist. Like Emma she decides against marriage, but marries just the same. Like Emma she suspects herself of loving one man and overlooks her love of another, misled, as Emma is, by a concealed engagement. Like Emma, she undergoes humiliation before she comes to a new understanding of her own behaviour, and like Emma she comes to this new self-awareness only through acknowledging her love for a man.

When Yonge decided to write about an arrogant and blundering but energetic and generous young woman frustrated in her desire for useful work by the conventional limitations and dullness of her environment— an ideal plot for a novel dealing with the contemporary issue of women's employment—she was evidently influenced, either consciously or unconsciously, by a close and intelligent reading of *Emma*. *The Clever Woman of the Family* functions as an exposé and explanation of Rachel's Emma-like mistakes, which follow from her attempts to find meaningful work for herself and to organize employment for working class women in her neighbourhood more equitably. It differs from *Emma*, however, most notably in the degree of punishment accorded the misdeeds of the central character: Emma spends a few days of private distress, whereas Rachel undergoes serious illness and public humiliation. Thus the novel is in many ways directly and wholeheartedly antifeminist. It can be read as the story of the errors of a youngish, not very attractive woman who dominates her more traditionally feminine mother, sister, and cousin. Under the influence of what Yonge calls "the spirit of the age" (337) and her own strong feelings of social concern and personal dedication, she attempts to organize a group promoting the employment of women. She is duped by a confidence trickster, Mauleverer; the children in the training school which she establishes are horribly abused (one dies of starvation, cruelty, and diphtheria); and she is publicly rebuked at Mauleverer's trial, feeling "as though all eyes were looking in triumph at that object of general scorn and aversion, a woman who had stepped out of her place" (253). She is rescued from her embarrassment and shame by marriage to the soldier-hero Alexander Keith, and by the end of the novel has seen the full error of her ways and found a proper outlet for her energies in the care of her husband and children. Unlike *The Daisy Chain*, where the energetic young woman is honoured by all who know her, this novel offers none of the consolations of fantasy: Rachel is firmly established as an embarrassing, charmless, and rather ridiculous young woman, and she is heavily punished for her offences against femininity.

The novel's strong antifeminist voice in the debate on women and work is also apparent in its barely-veiled allusions to the Langham Place Group and their activities for women's employment, to which Yonge was firmly opposed on principle. Rachel calls her women's work organization the Female Union for Lacemakers' Employment, using the initials FULE, until Alexander Keith gently points out that in Scottish (in Walter Scottish, anyway) this is the spelling of fool (145). Yonge was writing barely five years after the formation of the Society for the Promotion of the Employment of Women (SPEW) which also used its unfortunate initials, and she seems to have intended a little satire here. Certainly Rachel's enterprise is a provincial version of the Langham Place Group's work. Just as SPEW is connected with the *English Woman's Journal,* so Rachel hopes that her FUEE (she changes the L for Lacemakers to E for Englishwomen) will produce a *Journal of Female Industry* (199). Meanwhile she plans to send one of her reforming articles to a progressive publication that Yonge, satirizing the *English Woman's Journal,* names *The Englishwoman's Hobbyhorse* (89). Like the SPEW activists Rachel particularly wants to extend women's work from its conventional limitations: "Is it not a flagrant abuse," she asks, "that whether she have a vocation or not every woman of a certain rank, who wishes to gain her own livelihood, must needs become a governess?" (16). Her original ambition is to "become the founder of some establishment that might relieve women from the oppressive task-work thrown on them in all their branches of labour" (3). The institute that she founds, briefly fulfilling that ambition, trains little girls, who were originally expected to follow in the traditional local women's craft of lace-making, in "wood engraving and printing" (140), two of SPEW's most successful branches. Rachel also parallels the Langham Place feminists in her interest in female emigration and the employment opportunities it might offer (56)—Maria Rye had founded the Female Middle Class Emigration Society, a feminist organization, in 1862, and "the emigration idea spread rapidly among the feminist circles of the Social Science Association and the employment societies" (Hammerton 55).[16] The parallels between Rachel's fictional efforts and those of her historical London contemporaries are marked.

However, there is more to *The Clever Woman of the Family* than the story of "a woman who had stepped out of her place." It is not merely an exposé of the flaws of feminism, although it is that too. The novel's disturbing quality—the distress provoked by Rachel's story—arises partly from the complex presentation of Rachel and her errors. Certainly Yonge places Rachel as socially inept, heedless, ignorant, undisciplined, and overconfident, but she also carefully indicates that Rachel's plight is real and her exceptional energy, disinterestedness, and honesty admirable.[17] Yonge thus implies through this fictional instance that the problem of women and work is a real problem. For a start it is plain that Rachel's frustration is not just imaginary, and that her longing for "something to do" is not merely a response to boredom or a frivolous longing for anything to do but a refusal to ignore or passively accept the suffering she perceives. "Not a paper do I take up," she muses, "but I see something about wretchedness and crime, and here I sit with health, strength and knowledge, and able to do nothing, *nothing*—at the risk of breaking my mother's heart . . . here am I, able and willing, only longing to task myself to the uttermost, yet tethered down to the merest mockery of usefulness by conventionalities" (3). Rachel's concern with employment for women is not presented as in any way unfeminine, unworthy, or unnecessary; it would have been a suitable activity if suitably (religiously) done.

The narrowness of Rachel's circle, "a society well-born, but of circumscribed interests and habits," is also carefully established: unsurprisingly, Rachel finds herself "stranded on the ignorance of those who surrounded her" (6). Her longing to help is honoured by the two people whom Yonge creates as the mouthpieces of "right" opinion in the novel, the invalid writer Ermine Williams (a second, more clever, "clever woman") and Rachel's future husband, Alexander Keith. Ermine says that "there is something so noble about her that I cannot but believe that she will one day shake herself clear of her little absurdities" (172), while Keith's love is based on Rachel's "sincerity, generosity, and unselfishness" (271). He speaks of

> "the relief of meeting real truth and unselfishness! . . . I liked her for having no conventionalities, fast or slow, and especially for hating heroes! . . . how could I look on without feeling the nobleness that has never shifted blame from herself, but bowed, owned all, suffered—suffered—oh, how grievously!"
>
> (273)

However, Rachel's honesty, sincerity, and unselfishness do nothing to give her the feminine qualities of tact or charm. Her eventual sister-in-law, Bessie Keith (the third "clever woman"), acts as a foil for Rachel in this respect, for Bessie is selfish and manipulative but enchanting—convincingly enchanting, because she is intelligent and attractive enough to manipulate with skill, gaining her own ends and other people's good opinion at the same time. "Every other voice proclaims her winning, amiable, obliging, considerate, and devoted to the service of her friends" (190); the exception is her brother, who loves her but sees through her charm, recognizing her as "one of those selfish people who are infinitely better liked than those five hundred times their worth, because they take care to be always pleased" (188). Yonge describes and condemns in Bessie the manipulative cleverness that was and is commonly regarded as acceptable, even delightful in a girl or woman, while the novel itself validates Rachel's "charmless" qualities of energy, generosity, and truth.

When at the end of the novel Alexander and Rachel notice their bright little daughter's resemblance to Bessie (her aunt), Alexander says to his wife with an unchivalrous candour, "Rachel, such cleverness as that is a far more perilous gift to woman than your plodding intellectuality could ever be. God grant . . . that we may bring her up to your own truth and unselfishness" (367).

Not only are Rachel's good qualities honoured in the novel; her actions, despite their disastrous immediate results, are shown as effective, too. It is certainly because of Rachel's original efforts to provide women with work, misguided though they were, that a combined convalescent home and girl's training school for domestic service is eventually founded in her old home town—as she says, "I never hoped that such good fruit would rise out of my unhappy blunders" (365). Other women in this novel are also presented as working effectively. Although Rachel herself gives up her ambition to devote her life to philanthropy when she marries, she is introduced to a woman in London who "devoted herself to the care of poor girls to be trained as servants" (345), and who seems to be all that Rachel would like to have been. Ermine Williams, too, is presented as a gifted writer who is financially self-supporting, the assistant editor of a magazine, and an effective and virtuous woman: she provides this novel with a picture of Yonge's ideal of intellectual femininity—beautiful, elegant, religious, able, and active—her perfections marred only by the lameness that afflicts so many of Yonge's characters.[18] The novel ends with Alexander's encomium on Ermine:

> "If we are to show Una [their daughter] how intellect and brilliant power can be no snares, but only blessings, helping the spirits in infirmity and trouble, serving as a real engine for independence and usefulness, winning love and influence for good, genuine talents in the highest sense of the word, then commend me to such a Clever Woman of the family as Ermine [Williams] Keith." (367)

Ermine is an acceptable clever woman in being both effective and pious, by contrast with Rachel, who is portrayed as failing, not because as a woman she is incapable of effective action, but because of the inadequately religious basis of her attempts at effective action and her isolation from the male world. She is presented as falling short in both effectiveness and femininity because of spiritual inadequacy. Here Yonge gives a religious perspective to the debate on women and work; she is concerned with women's work in relation to their spiritual lives. As Keble's pupil, she deplored self-sufficiency—a commonly used Tractarian diagnostic term—as spiritually destructive, and she diagnoses self-sufficiency as Rachel's characteristic weakness and as especially deplorable in a young woman. However, the narrator provides a protracted analysis of gender relationships that suggests that this weakness is also especially easy to overcome in a young woman:

> a woman's tone of thought is commonly moulded by the masculine intellect, which, under one form or another, becomes the master of her soul. Those opinions once made her own, may be acted and improved upon, often carried to lengths never thought of by their inspirer, or held with noble constancy and perseverance even when he himself may have fallen from them, but from some living medium they are almost always adopted . . . And Rachel having been more than usually removed from the immediate influence of a superior man, had been affected by the more feeble and distant power, a leading that appeared to her the light of her independent mind; but it was not in the nature of things that, from her husband and his uncle, her character should not receive that tincture for which it had so long waited, strong and thorough in proportion to her nature.   (337-38)

Rachel's frustration and her gullibility are both analyzed as the result of lack of contact with educated males and lack of faith. Before she can act effectively, Rachel must realign herself with both the masculine and the spiritual world.

All the same, in this novel Yonge's definition of appropriate feminine effectiveness includes the capacity for action and achievement as well as energy, intelligence, generosity, sincerity and unconventionality. The treatment of such characters as Rachel and Ermine supports the case for enlarging the range of useful activities for middle-class women. Rachel's original condition of frustration suggests the need for such a change, and Ermine's original condition of achievement amidst difficulties suggests the feminine capacity for such change. Yet the inordinate sufferings that result from Rachel's misguided attempts to help—the suffering and death of the little girls, Rachel's own grief over her dead protégée, her long illness, and her public humiliation—indicate considerable anxiety over any challenge to the domestic role of woman.

Yonge acknowledged that an effective didactic writer avoids punishments that are too harsh for the character's crime ("Children's Literature" 310), but Rachel's misdeeds are severely treated. "A sense of failure was always good for Rachel" (316), comments the narrator, as if confidence were necessarily a fault in a woman. The function of marriage and motherhood as resolving the problems of both Rachel and Ermine shows the same discomfort at any questioning of domestic values. Yonge communicates both her intense concern and her unmistakable unease with her material, as, in *The Clever Woman of the Family*, she provides a Tractarian context for the contemporary debate over women and work.

VI

In no other novel does Yonge deal with this issue of women and work as an organizing principle as she does in *The Clever Woman of the Family*, which indeed expresses its period in its concentration on this subject. In only one later novel, *The Three Brides*, the subject of the next chapter, is she as closely and directly involved with issues of gender as she is in *The Clever Woman of the Family*. However, several of the later novels involve women characters with strong ambitions and successful careers, demonstrating Yonge's continuing concern with women's work; these characters are presented as exceptionally able and very much concerned with economic independence. A good example of Yonge's achieving women is the painter Geraldine (Cherry or Chérie) Underwood, in *The Pillars of the House*. By common consent Cherry is the most intelligent and amusing of a large and talented family of thirteen brothers and sisters. Yonge also presents her as an excellent painter. Art was becoming one of the more acceptable careers for a woman; 1069 women listed themselves as artists in the census of 1871, two years before Yonge published *The Pillars of the House* (Nunn 3), and despite the defensive hostility of many male artists, including the Royal Academicians (Nunn 46), women could take courses at the School of Design, later the Royal College of Art (Holcombe 62).[19]

Although Cherry admires her older brother Edgar, also a painter, and longs for his success, her work is, in fact, better than his, despite his advantages of longer training (Cherry has just a few weeks), of good health (Cherry has to have a foot amputated), and of unlimited free time (Cherry has domestic responsibilities and also helps her eldest brother edit the local newspaper). Thus in some ways the brilliant brother and sister echo the earlier Ethel and Norman May. When brother and sister both exhibit work for the first time at the Royal Academy, Edgar's painting of Brynhild amidst the flames is dismissed by the critics as the work of "a tyro in suspense between the Pre-Raffaelite [*sic*] and the Turneresque" (*Pillars* 2.115), whereas Geraldine's entries are highly praised and rapidly sold, and she goes on to win fame. Yonge depicts Geraldine as feeling a strong, if not totally unqualified, dedication to her work—"enough of the sacred fire to long to perfect her art" (351)—and a healthy ambition, comparatively rare emotions in contemporary fictional women. Cherry's ambition is acceptable because it is tempered by religious feeling:

> While striving to be satisfied with faithfully doing her best, [she] had so much wished for success as to make it a continual prayer, that the works of their hands might be prospered to both [herself and Edgar], and to feel it an effort honestly to add the clause, "If it be Thy will—if Thou see it good for us."
>
> (2: 107)

"The work of [her] hands" is also especially acceptable as a woman's work in being both religious and domestic in character: her Academy paintings portray an altar boy and her own pretty little sister.

Emotions even more rarely acknowledged and accepted in a fictional woman of the period than ambition are the desire to earn money and the pleasurable sense of power this gives; these feelings, too, Yonge, presumably understanding them from her own experience, depicts in Cherry. For instance, when Cherry receives a proposal of marriage, she is not pleased at the thought that marriage would have meant an end to paid work: "That was little recommendation. Her first rise out of uselessness gave her more exultation in its novelty than did even the exercise of her art, or the evidence of its success. There was something exquisite in the sense of power" (2.134). Indeed, Cherry feels that if she had no work she might have considered marriage, to relieve her brother of the expense of supporting her: paid work is a blessed and welcome economic alternative to marriage (2.135). Incidentally, by "uselessness" Cherry means financial uselessness, for she had already been of great use in domestic tasks, as her brother's editorial assistant, and as the younger children's teacher. Yonge acknowledges that money empowers and liberates, and that power and freedom are delightful to women as well as men.

Cherry's sister, Robina, shows a similar spirit. Robina (who, like Cherry, is presented as an admirable character) decides to continue working as a governess even after her eldest brother has inherited the family estate, Vale Leston. Her conventional (and Evangelical) neighbours are shocked: "no one worthy of the name of man will permit the ladies of his family to go out into the world for maintenance" (2.276), but her brother accepts that "the ladies of his family" make their own decisions on such matters. Robina is outspoken about the high value she places on her profession, ensuring that she is recognized as a governess because "I don't choose to seem ashamed of my vocation" (2.273). In *The Pillars of the House*, through characters such as Robina and Geraldine—and their cousin Marilda, a successful business woman—Yonge foregrounds a woman's right "to go out into the world for maintenance," her ability to work effectively and her obligation to use her talents—as long as her activities are understood as part of a religious life.

Of course, many of Yonge's working women work as teachers, paid and unpaid, as my comments on *The Daisy Chain* might suggest, and repeatedly these teachers are represented as women dedicated to their profession. Nowhere does Yonge portray a wretched governess in the Agnes Grey mould, but then she had not Anne Brontë's experience. The important point is that she sees the woman teacher as a dedicated professional. Indeed in *Womankind* she writes, "if she be a good governess and wise woman, it is as much her profession as law or medicine are those of men" (37). In *Hopes and Fears* (1860), indeed, Katherine Fennimore is represented as so dedicated that she half kills one of her pupils by driving her into a good Victorian brain fever from overwork, aggravated by a precocious love affair (and what seems to be an early case of anorexia nervosa). Alison Williams in *The Clever Woman of the Family* loves to teach, and so do Génevieve Durant in *The Young Stepmother*, and Robina and Wilmet Underwood in *The Pillars of the House*. Dolores Mohun, after her time at Cambridge, becomes a lecturer on the physical sciences (*The Long Vacation* and *Modern Broods*), "a leading woman in the instruction and formation of young minds" (*Long Vacation* 354). Ethel May of course is the supreme example of the teacher who loves to teach, although she is not a paid professional. Yonge consistently depicts governesses not as drudges driven to a wretched life of social exclusion by poverty but as dedicated experts, enjoying their work and their pupils; they are especially privileged because their work, like the writer's work, which Yonge also frequently presents as acceptable for women, usually leads them to or keeps them in the family setting that Yonge establishes as focal for both men and women.[20]

VII

Interestingly enough, despite her interest in dedicated working women, her lifelong Tractarianism and some first hand knowledge of the life of a sisterhood, Yonge shows comparatively little imaginative involvement with convent life. This fact perhaps indicates negatively her own deepest concerns as a writer. Yonge herself became an exterior sister of the Sisters of the Blessed Virgin Mary at Wantage after her mother's death in 1868 (Romanes 159); she contemplated taking full vows, but was dissuaded, probably on the grounds of the superior value of her literary work. Before this date she writes of sisterhoods with respect but only moderate interest, and considerable caution. She seems well aware of the suspicions many people felt for the sisterhoods, describing in *The Heir of Redclyffe* (1853) the mockery with which the little town of St. Mildred's treated the Misses Wellwood, who are to become the founders of a sisterhood. Even Dr. May, who is consistently presented as essentially right-thinking, is initially dubious about asking a sisterhood for help in a fever epidemic:

> Dr. May, who had at first, in his distrust of innovation, been averse to the importation—as likely to have no effect but putting nonsense into girls' heads, and worrying the sick poor—was so entirely conquered, that he took off his hat to them across the street, importuned them to drink tea with his daughters, and never came home without dilating on their merits. . . . The only counter demonstration he reserved to himself was that he always called them "Miss What-d'ye-call-her" and "Those gems of women," instead of Sister Katherine and Sister Frances. (*Trial* 10)

After spending more time with the Wantage sisterhood Yonge seems to take a slightly more positive and personal interest in the sisterhoods and to be less sensitive to public opinion, which in any case gradually became less hostile. In several novels (such as *The Three Brides*, in which members of a sisterhood nurse in a fever epidemic) sisterhoods play a background role, but in other novels especially of this later period, several more developed characters become closely involved in the life of the sisterhoods. In *The Pillars of the House* a character from a much earlier novel, *The Castle Builders*, Constance Somerville, reappears as Sister (later Mother) Constance. Her community takes in the lame Cherry Underwood (the painter) when she needs medical attention and nurses her after her foot is amputated, while Cherry's younger sister, Angela, becomes an associate of the community and as the novel ends is about to test her vocation. Yonge's last novel, *Modern Broods*, too, involves a young woman's vocation, while Angela Underwood, after a stormy religious and emotional career, finally reappears as a sister.

However, none of Yonge's clearly central female characters is described as seriously considering a possible religious vocation, and Yonge never explores very deeply the motivation of those who do. In *The Pillars of the House*, for instance, we have a far greater sense of Cherry's longing to be an artist and her preparation as an artist than we have of Angela's leanings towards a sisterhood, and indeed Angela is a far less developed and sympathetic character than Cherry. The world Yonge chooses to create and explore is a world of large families and of relationships within them. While as a woman she approved of the sisterhoods and honoured their work, as a novelist she was not imaginatively involved in them.

70

Families, relationships within families, duties that are usually fulfilled within a family setting, gender interactions in families, and talents that are either used or stifled within this setting—these are her imaginative concerns. The way this world of family relationship is constructed, the way it operates, accords entirely with the teaching on the primacy of family duty she absorbed in childhood and reiterated throughout her life. The mainspring of her imaginative creation is also the mainspring of her own behaviour. The sisterhoods, which unlike other professions involved complete withdrawal from family life, received her approval but did not attract her as a writer.

Yonge did not apparently consider joining a religious order until after the death of both her parents. Clearly she acted on her stated belief that home duties were given by divine providence and that they were therefore primary. For instance, Sister Constance takes on this identity rather than her worldly identity as Lady Herbert Somerville only as a widow. In fact, her husband is said to have bequeathed her like the rest of his property to the sisterhood ("her husband had left her, a childless widow, together with all else he had to leave, to the Sisterhood they had already founded" [*Pillars* 1.551]); he intended the Sisterhood "for Constance's work and comfort for life" (*Chaplet* 150).[21] Angela, in *Pillars*, and Paulina, in *Modern Broods*, both of whom enter sisterhoods, are younger members of their families (rather tiresome younger sisters) with no clear-cut family duties.

Another element in Yonge's attitude to the sisterhoods is the caution and reserve she imbibed with Keble's teaching. Keble was less active than Pusey in the founding of the sisterhoods, partly because he felt that the gossip about them (which he shrewdly predicted) would certainly do harm to the Tractarian cause. This is probably why (in 1844) he was reluctant to allow another woman who wanted to test her vocation to join Miss Moore, who had already moved to his parish for the sake of his spiritual direction (Battiscombe, *Keble* 248). Keble was also typically anxious that the pioneering sisters should neither be romanticized nor romanticize themselves. As ever, he was careful to avert any encouragement to spiritual pride or even normal self-confidence.[22] Such attitudes are reflected in Yonge's scrupulous avoidance of any tendency to romanticize sisterhoods, or indeed even to be explicit about them in her earlier novels. In such episodes as the restoration to religious uses of Rickworth Priory in *Heartsease* (1854) there is no explicit indication that the orphanage founded by Rickworth's owner, Emma Brandon, and its chapel are the basis of a future sisterhood. What Yonge carefully establishes,

71

however, is the unromantic fact that Emma, though good, is extremely silly and can commit herself thoroughly to her work only when chastened by an embarrassing entanglement with a fortune-hunter.

Such humiliation and suffering are inevitably salutary in a Yonge novel, and one related aspect of the new communities that she emphasizes is their discipline. She writes in *Womankind* of "the absolute need of the feminine nature for discipline and obedience" (5),[23] and certainly when her characters enter sisterhoods discipline is always a concern. When Angela Underwood first speaks to her brother of her ambitions, becoming a sister ranks with marrying a duke and going to the opera, presumably as equally effective escape routes from humdrum family life; but she recognizes that discipline is what she needs and wants to be in "a real strict nunnery" (*Pillars* 2.13); later Yonge comments that "the wild spirit craved for discipline as by a sort of instinct" (2.515). As the novel ends, Angela is about to become a postulant at St. Faith's sisterhood: it is "evidently the life she needs" (2.539). However, in the later linked novels, the unruly Angela is depicted as having failed to make her final vows at St. Faith's, as having flirted both with debauched aristocrats and Roman Catholicism, and as being a sort of unattached sister. When she is finally drowned (saving her beloved brother, Bernard) she is on her way back to Australia to make her vows, having at last accepted discipline.

VIII

Like others who felt oppressed by the usual expectations of women, Yonge, although she accepts much of the traditional lore of gender, rejects the non-religious conventional view of how women should spend their time. Like Florence Nightingale or Emily Davies, she opposes "the theory of society, that the whole duty of woman is to 'go gracefully idle'" (Davies 5). Yonge's contribution to the movement for enlarging the possibilities of activity for women—so essentially important to the women's movement in Victorian England—was not overt statement but fictional characters, situations, and resolutions. In her novels women are likely to have energy and talent, and are likely to be encouraged to use these energies and talents, and this likelihood generally increases throughout her long career. Some sweet, passive women in the more traditional feminine mould are presented for the admiration and edification of her readers, but Yonge on the whole is more likely to arouse interest and sympathy through female characters who are valued for their ability, honesty, integrity, or spiritual insight and who are placed in narratives that are not inevitably resolved in marriage. If the choices made by these women are sometimes presented as based on self-abnegation, these characters do not deny their need for work, and they make sure that they fulfill that need. They work effectively in a range of positions, paid and unpaid; they have the innate qualities (the gifts and the perseverance) that enable them to work effectively; and above all they are committed to their work. Yonge is profoundly unsympathetic to many of the assumptions of the women who were working for women's employment in the 1860s, but she shares many of their goals.

CHAPTER THREE

"The Monstrous Regiment of Women": *The Three Brides* (1876) and Women's Political and Legal Status

Between 1874 and 1877 Yonge, as editor of *The Monthly Packet*, ran concurrently two of her own works, the essay series *Womankind* (1874-77) and a novel, *The Three Brides* (1874-76). As her titles suggest, Yonge at this period was directly engaged with questions of women's roles and duties. The chapter headings of *Womankind* include "Woman's Status," "Views and Opinions," "Money-Making," "Strong-Minded Women," and "Authority," while *The Three Brides* deals with women's roles not only in marriage but also in active public and political life: all the women characters in this novel are placed by their reactions to the current debate over the status of women, a debate that literally and figuratively provides a centre for the novel, as shown below. Yonge, like most novelists of the period, on the whole avoids identifiable contemporary names, places, dates or issues; nevertheless, both these carefully argued and deliberately conservative works are demonstrably written in the context of a new phase and a new urgency in the debate over women. The increasing agitation over women's political and legal rights in the period preceding and for many years following the Reform Act of 1867 and the Married Women's Property Act of 1870 provided a new focus for the women's movement: education and work necessarily remained important questions, but the public debate now focused with renewed energy on political and legal issues.

This new intensity of concern with the position of women colours numerous texts of the period. *Middlemarch* (1871-72) is the best-known example. Many of Eliot's original reviewers read her novel and evaluated it in relation to the woman question (Blake 285)—partly, no doubt, because (as with critics a century later) that was where their own attention was directed. Eliot's response to the preoccupations of her own society is displaced onto the social and political agitations preceding the first Reform Act of 1832 and the more general questions of women's aspirations, position and education. Yonge, however, like Trollope (in *Is He Popenjoy?*, which is almost precisely contemporary with *The Three*

Brides) treats these problems more directly with portrayals of women's rights workers, discussions of women's rights issues, and an extensive and topical treatment of the proper relationship between husband and wife.[1] Less directly, she explores the negative effect on women of the perpetual frustrations and restrictions involved in the domestic and social subordination which Yonge believes to be God-given.

This chapter places *The Three Brides* as part of the context of an unprecedented concern with the practical issues of gender equity; it comments on how Yonge's continuing refinement and redefinition of the concept of femininity involves a combination of unswerving anti-feminism and complex understanding of the motivations of feminist women. Like *The Clever Woman of the Family* six years earlier, this novel is almost exclusively concerned with gender roles. This time, however, Yonge explores gender not in relation to appropriate outlets for women's energies but rather in relation to the issue of the role of women in marriage and also to contemporary political movements. Like *The Clever Woman of the Family* again, while celebrating the traditional domestic role of women this novel also shows the equivocal relation between femininity and power. Yonge's polemics about gender in *Womankind* deny that women are oppressed in her society, asserting that the single woman's only possible deprivation is the vote, which would be in any case a burden, while also justifying current legislation regarding married women: "our position depends entirely upon what we are in ourselves," she claims (236). *The Three Brides* does not imply that women are power-less: it contrasts the "lawful supremacy" (48) of men with the "natural supremacy" (153) of women—presumably the same power that for some women comes from "what [they] are [themselves]." The novel, however, shows the suffering caused by the oppression of wives, daughters and sisters that Yonge denies in her essays. It suggests not only the folly of transgressing gender codes but also the pain of submission to gender codes: as in *The Clever Woman of the Family* the narrative explores the apparently inevitable frustration and suffering of women.

I

The main indications of the renewed excitement about women's rights at this period can be outlined rapidly. The terms of the Reform Act of 1867 qualified many more adult males to vote in parliamentary elections. As more men became enfranchised, necessarily more enfranchised men were less "qualified" according to established concepts of qualification— less experienced in public life through the traditional rights and duties

75

of property-owning and through the traditional education of the privileged male. The force of the contrast between the newly enfranchised men and all women, automatically disenfranchised, however great their individual abilities, experience, learning, or property, was powerful: inevitably it drove many women and men alike to consider the question of women's suffrage. Lydia Becker wrote in 1867:

> To individual men the law says, "All of you whose rental reaches the proscribed standard shall have your political existence recognized. You may not be clever nor learned; possibly you do not know how to read and write." . . . But to individual women the law says, "It is true that you are persons with opinions, wants and wishes of your own . . . and that your intelligence is not inferior to that of great numbers of male voters . . . but . . . we will not allow you to have the smallest share in the government of the country." (*VF* 61)

Between 1865 and 1866 fifteen thousand women signed the Women's Suffrage Petition requesting that women be given the same rights as men; John Stuart Mill, whose election as MP in 1865 is also an important marker in the suffrage movement, presented this petition to an unsympathetic Parliament in 1866 (Bauer and Ritt 207, 217). In 1867, during the debate over the Reform Bill, Mill moved an amendment that the bill use the word "person" rather than "man"; again the amendment lost, 196-83 (Bauer and Ritt 217). Despite the failure of Mill's amendment, after the passage of the bill women continued to test the legal implications of its wording. R.M. Pankhurst provided in his essay, "The Right of Women to Vote Under the Reform Act of 1867" (*Fortnightly Review* 1868, 250-54), "a short statement about some of the grounds and reasoning in accordance with which it is contended that under the 'Representation of the People Act of 1867' all women who are *sui juris* and possess the necessary qualifications are entitled to vote" (Bauer and Ritt 222). Accordingly about five thousand women property-owners attempted to register as voters (Hollis 7), until the legal decision disqualifying all women in the "Chorlton v. Lings" case of 7 November 1868, in the Court of Common Pleas (Rover 32). Meanwhile in 1867 Lydia Becker had initiated the Manchester Women's Suffrage Committee; similar groups were started in London, Bristol, Birmingham, and Edinburgh, and these committees were the basis of a national organization, the National Society for Women's Suffrage, which Mill describes as "a numerous and active society organized and managed by women, for the . . . limited object of obtaining the political franchise" (29). In 1870 a Suffrage Bill actually went through its second reading in the House of Commons by 124 votes to 91; a couple of days later the Queen wrote to Gladstone, then Prime

Minister, deploring "this dangerous and unchristian and unnatural cry and movement of women's rights" (Bauer and Ritt 247). Whether or not through Royal influence, the bill was killed in the committee stage by the determined opposition of Mr. Gladstone (who was incidentally a Tractarian sympathizer). Despite this discouragement, the suffrage movement grew steadily throughout the 1870s, and between the passing of the 1867 and the 1884 Reform Acts at least eleven divisions of the House of Commons involved the question of women's suffrage (Brian Harrison 28).

In these years, as the struggle for parliamentary votes intensified, women achieved a stronger political presence at the local level. The Municipal Franchise Act of 1869 entitled all women rate-payers to vote in local elections: "the question passed through the House without a dissentient word, causing surprise and excitement of a quiet sort and much pleasure to the real friends of the Cause," Lydia Becker wrote to Barbara Leigh Smith Bodichon (Strachey 205). In 1870 women won the right to vote for the new School Boards; in 1875 this right extended to Poor Law Boards, in 1888 to County Councils and in 1894 to Parish and District Councils (Pugh 13). In the first School Board election of 1870 four women were elected as members of various School Boards—Lydia Becker in Manchester, Flora Stevenson in Edinburgh, and Emily Davies and Elizabeth Garrett in London. In the later 1870s women were also elected as Poor Law Guardians, the first elected being Martha Merrington in 1875 (Strachey 206); during the remaining years of the century the number of women serving in local politics in various capacities steadily increased, a significant move towards full suffrage.

The vigorous campaigns to change the status of women at this period were of course directed not only at women's political position but also their legal status, especially the position of married women.[2] At the beginning of Victoria's reign, under the common law,[3] a married woman had no legal rights over her own person, her property, her earnings, or her children, and yet divorce was virtually impossible for her. "The manifold evils occasioned by the present law, by which the property and earnings of the wife are thrown into the absolute power of the husband," were protested in a petition for the reform of the married women's property law presented to Parliament on 14 March 1856 and signed by Elizabeth Gaskell, Elizabeth Barrett Browning, and twenty-two other distinguished women (Holcombe, *Wives* 237-38). Similar agitation both inside and outside Parliament, most notably perhaps the eloquent protests of Caroline Norton,[4] surrounded the discussions of both the Married Women's Property Bill and the Divorce Bill of 1857; the latter was passed but not the former. Thus this phase of the movement for legal reform ended in frustration, but all the same Bessie Parkes saw in the work of the Married Women's Property Committees "a real beginning for the women's movement" (Herstein 78). The debate over marriage was renewed in 1868 with an energetic two-year campaign to change the law regarding married women's property, involving 35,000 pamphlets, 142 petitions to the House of Commons and 70 petitions to the House of Lords (*FL* 117). A Married Women's Property Act was passed in 1870, but this "legislative abortion" (Holcombe, *Wives* 183) pleased nobody; the campaign for change continued, and parliamentary debates on this subject are recorded for 1873, 1874, 1877, 1878, 1879, 1880, and 1881. Finally in 1882 a satisfactory Act was passed by which married women were treated as *femes soles* in regard to property—"a great measure of justice advantageous to all classes of the community, and calculated to raise the dignity and stability of the marriage relationship in this country," according to the victorious Married Women's Property Committee (Holcombe, *Wives* 204).

Thus in the late 1860s and throughout the 1870s, women's roles in parliamentary politics, in local politics, and their legal status in marriage were continually under public discussion. Interest in these topics is also evident in the publications of the period. Non-specialist periodicals, from *Punch* and the *Saturday Review* to *The Westminster Review*, devoted many pages of invective, ridicule, or argument to these issues. In 1869 alone, notable relevant publications included not only Mill's *The Subjection of Women* but also an important collection of essays edited by Josephine Butler, *Woman's Work and Woman's Culture*, and two works by Frances Power Cobbe, *Why Women Desire the Franchise*, and *Criminals, Idiots, Women, and Minors: Is the Classification Sound?* In the same year Barbara Leigh Smith Bodichon published *Reasons for and against the Enfranchisement of Women*, as well as reissuing her influential little book, *A Brief Summary in Plain Language of the Most Important Laws Concerning Women, Together with a Few Observations Thereon* (originally published in 1854), revising it, according to Herstein, to reflect her conviction that suffrage was of prime importance to women (167). In 1870 Lydia Becker, who had first made her name through an article on "Female Suffrage" in the *Contemporary Review* in March 1867, founded the *Woman's Suffrage Journal*, which she also edited and which published all parliamentary speeches made on the subject (Bauer and Ritt 219), while the *English Woman's Review* continued to publish relevant articles throughout the 1870s and 1880s. On a different level and with a different agenda, Eliza Lynn Linton's virulent "Girl of the Period" essays, which continued in the

Saturday Review until 1877, are symptomatic of popular antifeminist journalism. The general excitement in the period over the question of women's rights is inescapable, and Charlotte Yonge's own contribution is exceptionally full, forthright, and discomfiting.

II

"The Monstrous Regiment of Women" is the title of the chapter which lies at the centre of *The Three Brides*, both physically and intellectually: it features a set-piece in which Yonge engages with "the great question" of "the Equality of the Sexes" (158), assembling most of the central characters for a drawing-room debate on the subject.[5] Yonge's epigraph for this chapter, "Descend, my Muse," plays not only with the name of the American lecturer who speaks for emancipation—Clio—but also presumably with Yonge's sense that this kind of organized discussion expressing divergent opinions on an important political issue is far beyond the normal scope of her writing. While her dialogue is usually convincing, her forte lies in the spontaneous and playful exchange between family members or friends rather than in this kind of focused discussion. The deliberate and uncharacteristic explicitness of her engagement with the question of the status of women indicates Yonge's sense of the urgency of this issue; a far briefer commentary, equally conspicuous in its polemical topicality, is the description of Geraldine Underwood's drawings of women's place inside and outside the church in *The Pillars of the House* (see Chapter Two, above), which dates from the same period. The stated readership of Yonge's journal, *The Monthly Packet*, after all, was young women—"young girls, or maidens or young ladies" (Battiscombe, *Yonge* 67)—who inevitably will have recognized their personal involvement with issues that directly affect their present and future lives.

The Three Brides as a whole addresses gender concerns, but the debate as such addresses the fundamental issues of women's innate and sexually determined abilities and how these abilities affect their social position. Yonge's feminists and antifeminists in fact express much the same essentialist view of gender: they agree that men and women are essentially different and that in many ways women are morally superior to men. Feminist and antifeminists both believe that "generous forbearance, patience, fortitude, and self-renunciation, belong almost naturally to the true wife and mother and are her great glory" (161), just as Yonge herself asserts in *Womankind* that "the graces of humility, meekness, and submission . . . are the true strength and beauty of womanhood" (240). The fictional feminists in *The Three Brides* use this assumption of superiority to argue for women's emancipation, and Levine asserts that in fact the assumption of women's moral superiority significantly affected the various feminist campaigns:

> If women's purity made them the natural custodians of religious teachings and values, then their effect in public life could only be uplifting. The sentiment of moral superiority became the leading edge of many women's rights campaigns in this period, not only in the more obvious area of sexuality but in more overtly parliamentary concerns as well. (*VF* 13)

However, the antifeminists base their case on their fear that, with emancipation, women would lose their unique qualities "by self-assertion as the peer in power" (161). The antifeminists see women as relative: they value women's moral virtues in so far as they inspire and ennoble men, expressing the fear that equality might mean the loss of women's miraculous capacity "to purify the atmosphere wherever they go," because of the "hardening and roughening process" (162) that they would undergo if they were treated in the same way as men. The unfeminine woman created by this "roughening process" would then fail in her relationships with the male: "she will be no restraint on his bad habits, no curb on the coarseness of his nature. All she will be is an unsexed creature, lowering the whole standard of womanhood, and therewith of human nature" (*Womankind* 107). As Clio says, "one man says she is for his pleasure, another for his servant, and you for—for his refinement. You all would have us adjectives" (162). The fictional American lecturer here echoes the actual English feminist Frances Power Cobbe who in 1869 had written of "the types of Woman considered as an Adjective" (6-7).[6] What Clio wants is acceptance, not as an "adjective" but as "a substantive" (162). *The Three Brides* as a whole advocates the perpetuation of the adjectival status of women.

Women's superior but fragile virtues are stressed by a man, the Rector, Julius Charnock. The most vocal woman antifeminist, Joanna Bowater, is more hostile to her feminist hosts and less placatory. She questions women's intellectual abilities, arguing that women have never produced any work "of equal honour and permanence with that of men" (159), denying the opposition argument that the disparity arises because woman's "training has been sedulously inferior" (159) by asserting (what was Yonge's own view of history) that women were well-educated in Italy in the cinquecento and in Elizabethan England but even so produced nothing of intrinsic value. Apparently Joanna is here the voice of her author, who in *Womankind* questions women's achievements in the same terms: "mentally, where has the woman ever been found who produced any great or permanent work? What woman has written an oratorio or an epic, or built a cathedral? It is not lack of education. . . . The difference can only be in the mental texture" (233). The feminists' Millian assertion that there is no evidence for judging woman's capacities on the basis of her achievements "in her down-trodden state" is taken as a rejection of "all arguments from proved facts" (160); and it is on the basis of these "proved facts"—women's limited achievements under patriarchy —together with biblical authority that the antifeminists' argument finally prevails—at least in their own eyes and in those of their chronicler. Joanna is gleefully described as "the fittest memberess for the future parliament" (163) as they drive home.

The debate covers women's abilities and their equality, but it does so through questions of general entitlement and desirability rather than through specific issues, such as representation, employment, or property rights. Yonge would probably regard overt discussion of such issues as unfeminine and inappropriate. The debate provides a forum in which the basis of the opposition to women's rights can be strongly asserted, and it obviates any accusation of prejudice by making an educated woman voice the strongest opposition to equality.[7]

III

The debate makes explicit general arguments that run through the novel as a whole. The entire plot of *The Three Brides* hinges on the issue of the status of women, arising as it does from two events, one domestic and one public. The first is the arrival at Compton Poynsett, a large country house, of the new brides of three of the five Charnock (Charnock Poynsett) brothers, the sons of its owner, the widowed and paralysed Mrs. Charnock Poynsett;[8] the second is the fire which devastates the neighbouring country town, Willansborough, two days after their arrival. Both these events trigger narrative sequences that are used to promote the discussion and enactment of attitudes to gender roles. The contrasting marriages obviously prompt a discussion of women's roles in marriage—of how in a patriarchal society new wives learn to identify with the interests of their husbands' rather than their fathers' families. The fire in its turn involves local government and social issues, concerns that Yonge relates directly to the question of the emancipation of women; reflecting contemporary probability, she portrays the most active participants in local issues as being also feminists (hence the debate discussed above).

While Yonge's opposition to any change in women's status is unswerving, she nevertheless provides some of the more convincing portraits of

81

women's rights workers of the period. A comparison with Trollope's contemporary work is to the point. While both writers opposed the women's movement in their non-fiction (Yonge's essays of 1877, in *Womankind*; Trollope's lecture of 1868, "Higher Education for Women"), their fictitious feminists are quite different. Trollope's treatment of his suffragists in *Is He Popenjoy?* is simply hostile—even more so than in the earlier *He Knew He Was Right* (1869): the Baroness Banman is physically repellent, stupid, and grasping, and Dr. Olivia Q. Fleabody is almost equally ridiculous.[9] Yonge's women activists, on the other hand, have a different and more complex function and are accordingly more complex creations. Her engagement with gender definitions leads to a fuller exploration: her feminists have not automatically discarded their femininity. While Trollope's American Wallachia Petrie in *He Knew He Was Right* is a "republican virago," Yonge's American lecturer, Clio Tallboys—more like Trollope's friend Kate Field than any of his own creations—is elegant, beautiful, domestically competent, and married to an adoring Harvard Professor. She is "one of those women of resource whose practical powers may well inspire the sense of superiority" (158). Even though one Charnock brother, the conservative MP Raymond, may in a fit of irritation describe her as "an American mountebank of a woman" whose lectures are "absurd trash" (148-49), the narrative makes it clear that she cannot be dismissed so easily. In *Womankind* Yonge briskly dismisses women lecturers as seeing the world as "a sort of bee-hive, all the males drones, and the single sisters doing all the work" (239); when the demands of fiction force her to imagine the reality of such a lecturer, her presentation is less simplistic.

Clio's English counterpart, Bessie Duncombe, is drawn more fully. She has shed some of the properly feminine qualities of the nurturing woman, but retains other indications of gender identity. Her domestic arrangements are those of a more realistically drawn Mrs. Jellyby—her children are neglected, her house untidy, even her geraniums leafless—but all the same she is an affectionate wife and an attractive woman, and moreover humane as well as clever, energetic, and sincere. In the credibly presented series of catastrophes that follow the terrible fire in Willansborough—the destruction of factories leads to unemployment and to rebuilding with inadequate drainage arrangements, which leads to water pollution, which leads to a fever epidemic—Bessie is consistently the most effective leader. Thus after the fire wipes out the paper factories which are the main local employers, she organizes effective alternative employment for the hundred-odd women thrown out of work. Even Raymond is reluctantly forced to support this "very sensible practical arrangement" (55), although he deplores her addressing a public meeting to advocate her plan. Mrs. Duncombe also insists that an effective drainage system be installed before the town is reconstructed, and when after the official rejection of her proposal its partial implementation leads to contamination of the wells, she is the only effective worker in the resulting fever epidemic, apart from the Anglican nuns and clergy.

Bessie Duncombe is in fact presented as a more intelligent and practical version of Rachel Curtis in *The Clever Women of the Family*, but like Rachel she learns through the deadly consequences of her action. She is, like Rachel, imagined as an energetic but misguided women. She is honoured for taking action, and portrayed as effective and as more admirable than the more conventionally acceptable worldly women of the novel, though less admirable than the unquestioningly domestic women of the novel. As a devoted Tractarian, Yonge directs her approval to the dedicated rather than the merely conventional. Yonge accounts for Bessie Duncombe's feminism as the attempt of a neglected but intelligent young woman to find a worthy set of values. Bessie says of herself, "when I was set free of my school at Paris, and married Bob three months later, I hadn't three ideas in my head beyond horses and balls and soldiers. It has all come with life and reading." The narrator comments, "and a very odd 'all' it was . . . [but] the 'gospel of progress' was . . . the first she had ever really known, and became a reaching forward to a newly-perceived standard of benevolence and nobleness" (154). While the "gospel of progress" in this context is obviously contrasted (to its detriment) with the Christian gospel, it represents a spiritual choice and is moreover a properly feminine spiritual choice in that it involves "benevolence and nobility"—the doctrine of service and self-sacrifice which as a Tractarian Yonge sees as especially appropriate to all middle-class women.

The women in this novel, as has been suggested, are judged by their reaction to the contemporary women's movement. The women who have most completely internalized their gender role are naturally not interested in the question of emancipation because they completely accept their traditional positions in the church and in marriage. Those who care seriously about women's issues are presented as admirable in certain ways, making their first steps along the path of middle-class Christian femininity, though misguided through circumstances. The harshest judgment is reserved for those who are attracted to the women's cause for selfish, frivolous, or worldly reasons. Their presence in the novel suggests the nature of Yonge's doubts about the movement. The involvement of Raymond's wife, Cecil, for instance, arises from "the spirit of rivalry and

83

opposition" (154) and the need for assertion in her difficult new life: in relation to the debate over women "all that she wanted was her own way and opposition" (153). Lady Tyrrell, a beautiful and unscrupulous widow, is "only drawn into the controversy [about the emancipation of women] as a matter of amusement" (115)—she delights and excels in trouble-making. Miss Moy, the "fast" girl, is interested merely because "I don't see why we shouldn't have our own way just as well as the men" (132). She cares only for "the boisterous side of emancipation" (154), and when she finally elopes with a vulgar and unreliable man from the local training stables she credits "the rights of women" with inspiring her actions (287).[10] In her case, "feminism" is seen both as a fault against gender and as an indication of her lower social status.

These women are unwomanly not because of their interest in women's rights but because of their self-interest; self-absorption is the essential fault against femininity in Yonge's fiction, and thus she equates true middle-class femininity in certain ways with Christian spiritual values. She regards the emancipation of women as potentially disruptive of the social hierarchy and therefore dangerous. But in *The Three Brides*, as in *The Clever Woman of the Family*, her serious religious concern leads her to perceive a serious, disinterested concern—even with women's rights—and a commitment to service as promising indications of a movement away from the merely conventional and selfish life of a prosperous middle-class woman and towards moral activity, and thus ultimately towards spiritual activity—the "meritorious action" (*Womankind* 214) that is so strongly emphasized in Tractarian teaching. Mrs. Duncombe, who takes the movement seriously, devotes all her energies to "strive her utmost to get the work done" (132) and is respected accordingly. By the end of the novel she is a committed Christian—though the fact that she becomes a Roman Catholic rather than a Yongean Anglo-Catholic may speak for her author's fears that some early disadvantages are never completely overcome.

IV

The issue of women's rights in *The Three Brides* is directly connected with women's service, and in this the novel reflects its period. Women's power to choose was directly related to women's willingness to serve, especially in local politics. For instance, Lydia Becker's involvement in local school board politics was certainly connected with her suffrage agenda in that she was proving herself as a politically and socially responsible woman, and thus supporting her argument that women are politically and socially responsible persons. Jane Rendall indeed suggests that "in Britain there is a strong case for suggesting that social issues—employment, sanitary reform, the reform of state institutions—had priority over the political issue of the vote in generating a feminist movement" (272). As noted above, local government and social welfare on the local level were areas in which women were gaining power at this period, as they became entitled to vote for various local forms of government and began to act as officers for local boards and committees. Yonge responds to this phenomenon of the 1870s with some predictable ambivalence: women's service was acceptable, but the related potential of independent power was another matter.

In *The Three Brides* women's involvement in local issues is crucial to the plot, the specific issue being water supplies and sanitation. As Alethea Hayter points out, Yonge frequently uses the Victorian concern with problems of drainage and clean water supply as a narrative device in her novels (840). In *The Trial* (1864) bad drainage leads to a lethal epidemic in Stoneborough; in *The Young Stepmother* (1861) fevers resulting from bad drainage kill off the mother and six of the children of the central family. Here again in *The Three Brides* (1876) drainage is of vital importance but there is a difference: women are presented as actually working together in order to save the town and make it more healthy. The original proposal that effective drainage be installed before the town is reconstructed after the fire comes from Mrs. Duncombe, and when this proposal is turned down it is she who organizes a partial drainage scheme, with the financial backing of one of the three brides, the rebellious Cecil. When the inadequate drainage system pollutes the wells and causes a fever outbreak, Mrs. Duncombe's organization is properly exonerated and the town council blamed: "the responsibility rested, not with those who had done all within their power or knowledge for the welfare of their tenants, but with those whose indifference on the score of health had led them to neglect all sanitary measures" (238).

However, Yonge's treatment of the effects of Mrs. Duncombe's actions seems to imply an unresolved intellectual conflict in regard to women and service. By implication women are too ignorant and incompetent to be involved in public affairs without disaster, and yet they are public-spirited, effective and sympathetic to the need for social action: Mrs. Duncombe is both guilty and not guilty of causing the outbreak of fever. This paradox is implicit in the conservative notion of separate spheres; if for a woman citizenship depends not on political power but on social service (Brian Harrison 59), then by implication women are both responsible and irresponsible—responsible enough for essential service to the community but not responsible enough for the exercise of political power within that community. The paradox of women's service was of course further entrenched by the fact that the boundaries between public and private became obscured in some areas at this period, as government at all levels was reluctantly forced to intervene in matters that had previously been regarded as private concerns: "sanitation and housing, water supplies and the control of disease, all became subject to government directive in some way during the nineteenth century" (*FL* 131). Because all these subjects had previously been areas of private life, of household management, inevitably it seemed natural that women should concern themselves with them when they became part of public life. As early as 1861 the Ladies' Sanitary Association had already been formed and was filing its fourth report (Hollis 241-42). In writing of this ambiguous area Yonge reflects its ambiguity. In representing women's public service at the local level she simultaneously communicates admiration and suspicion.

V

The question of women's political and legal rights obviously directly affects their private as well as their public lives, especially at a period of constant debate about marriage laws. To ask what a woman should do with her life—Alice Vavasour's famous question in Trollope's *Can You Forgive Her?*—"in the mid-nineteenth century meant, in fiction at least, the consideration of a woman's position in relation to marriage," writes Kate Flint ("Introduction" xv). Similarly, Levine writes of the widespread recognition of marital status as "the defining feature which shaped the lives of women, willy-nilly, from cradle to grave" (*FL* 106). Yonge's novel about women's position thus inevitably focuses not only on the general debate about equality in relation to the innate qualities of women, and on the question of service in relation to political representation, but more specifically and more intensively on marriage. Her overall position in regard to women and marriage is that of the book of Genesis, and she quotes at the beginning of *Womankind* God's words to the fallen Eve: "thy desire shall be to thy husband and he shall rule over thee" (4). The church and especially High Church functionaries were taking a strong opposing line in the then-current debate over the changing legal status of married women—after all, divorce had been a matter of ecclesiastical law until the Divorce Act of 1857, which Keble had described as "a bill for legalizing adultery" (Mare and Percival 122)—and Yonge takes a similarly conservative hierarchical position. Her opposition to the energetic campaign to separate wives' financial interests from those of their husbands is expressed strongly, but not in explicitly political or legal terms; she writes rather of the complex personal and family relationships which shape and are shaped by social structures. While the proponents of reform to the law applying to married women might be regarded as arguing for a weakening of patriarchal power in marriage, the marriages imagined in *The Three Brides* are presented in terms of an unquestionably patriarchal and patrilinear institution, and Yonge habitually invokes biblical authority to support this view of the husband as "God-given authority" (*Womankind* 183). The issue in each of the three marriages is how the wife will come "to forget her own people and her father's house" (281), as Yonge writes, echoing the words of the Psalmist (Psalm 45:10). The story of each of the three brides tells of how she comes to discard her lifelong habits and assume those of her husband's family.

All three brides of the title are represented as at first strongly resisting absorption into their husbands' family and its values, but all are driven eventually to recognize that this absorption is essential for a happy marriage. Cecil, the unhappy bride of the eldest son (Raymond the MP), is in fact widowed before she comes to accept her new family. Cecil's confusion and resistance is represented as insubordination: she cannot tolerate her role as daughter-in-law to the powerful, widowed materfamilias, Mrs. Charnock Poynsett and (not without justification) sees her mother-in-law as a rival in love rather than as a new parent. Nor can Cecil give up her belief in the superiority of the code of her family of origin. The narrative thus suggests that she, rather than her unloving husband, is to blame for the failure of her married life. The happiness of her eventual second marriage is seen as based on a paradoxical liberation-through-conquest: her resistance is overcome as she is at last "entirely conquered by the tyrant love" and thus ceases to be "the slave of her own way" (336). The suggestion that married happiness is necessarily founded on the woman's complete surrender is foregrounded by the position of this statement at the very end of the novel, as the culmination of its disquisition on marriage.

Cecil's resistance to her mother-in-law and her domestic position is described with some asperity and little sympathy, but her suffering in her loveless first marriage through frustration, wounded pride, and jealousy is strongly presented, as a "heart-sickness she had never known or supposed possible" (165). Anne, the second bride, is similarly placed in a wretched position in her husband's family, and is similarly implied to be at fault until she is happily reconciled to this position. However, once again the suffering of the young wife in making the adjustment to her new position is strongly realised, and her painful isolation in the family is foregrounded: her naval officer husband, Captain Miles Charnock, dispatches her to England while he is away on a long voyage, sending her away from her home on a busy South African farm to a great English house of the leisured classes, where she arrives wretchedly ill, having miscarried a much-wanted baby on the journey. She is morally as well as emotionally isolated, for after her puritanical and hardworking farm upbringing, the religious and social habits of the English Tractarian landed gentry seem appallingly worldly to her. Yonge works carefully to indicate the full wretchedness of the young wife's situation. Yet Anne's eventual resignation to her new family role—the care of her mother-in-law, the honouring of Tractarian religious observances, and her responsibilities as an MP's wife after Miles takes over his dead brother's constituency—is presented as the acceptance of her proper role as a Christian wife.

The third bride has a happier story: Rosamond's adjustment to her position in her husband's family is less difficult because it is the consequence not of religious principles but of emotional security arising from her strong and unquestioning identification with the feminine role as loving wife and mother, from the presence of her loving husband, and from her own pleasure in helping others. The narrative thus implies that the truly feminine woman, the woman accepting of her gender role, will make such adjustments naturally and thus be a spontaneously religious wife: the acceptance of gender roles buttresses patriarchal institutions. All the same, Lady Rosamond, the wife of the Reverend Julius Charnock, is slow in accepting wifely subordination, not because like Anne she is too austerely religious, but because she is too frivolously worldly. Partly out of family loyalty she adheres to the "ramshackle easy-going ways" (197) of her father (both an earl and an army officer) and dresses and behaves like a colonel's daughter rather than a rector's wife. She finally gives up her balls, visits, and race-going when she is brought face to face with the full extent of the corruption and damage—drunkenness, violence, sexual license, and financial ruin—wrought by the local race meeting. She vows, "I'll never never go anywhere again" (218) and proceeds to devote herself to the feminine roles of mother, wife, sister, daughter and lady bountiful, the ease of her capitulation made credible by the pleasure she takes in these roles. Meanwhile her mother-in-law has already decided that Julius is too much in love with Rosamond "for the good of his lawful supremacy" (48).

"Lawful supremacy" is very much the issue in this novel. These difficult adjustments by the woman to the customs of the husband's family are presented as the proper mode of adjustment to the mutual demands of marriage. In articulating the necessity for a proper wife to accept the change of position within patriarchal structures that she undertakes in marriage, Yonge also displays the pain involved in this acceptance. All three young women suffer as brides, not through any physical defloration but through the power of new social constraints, and through the strength of the demands made on them to conform, to adapt, and to re-educate themselves. The foregrounding of this pain forces a sense of the compulsion to adjust. Thus Yonge presents unflinchingly the consequences of the ideal of wifely self-sacrifice which she puts forward in *Womankind*: "the true kind of wife, whose great work and delight in life is to be the complement of her husband, doing for him all those things that he need not do for himself—sparing him all vexatious details—giving him her sympathy in all his desirable pursuits, and exerting herself to share whatever he likes her to share in, and adapting herself to his moods with ready tact" (188). The concrete presentation of relationships in fiction communicates the discomfort easily glossed over in presenting an abstract ideal.

VI

The Three Brides is an uncomfortable novel, even more so than *The Clever Woman of the Family*; it involves frustration, failure, difficulty, and confinement. In both novels, which because they focus explicitly on gender are most explicitly antifeminist, Yonge seems compelled to confront her readers with a rigid and frequently painful definition of femininity. *The Pillars of the House* (1873), which comes between *The Clever Woman of the Family* (1865) and *The Three Brides* (1876) and is far less focused on issues of gender, is full of men and women who despite poverty, heartache, and even crippling illness, are exceptionally active and successful: they run newspapers, shops, and businesses, write and sell poems, paint and sell pictures, sing well, teach well, marry well, and look good. *Magnum Bonum* (1879), the novel subsequent to *The Three Brides*, is concerned with gender roles and definitions only to a minor extent, and it, too, is full of effective and talented women and men. In *The Three Brides*, which deals with the roles of women in marriage and in society at large, our imaginations are directed not to action or achievement—few of the characters are professionally active and none of them especially talented—but rather to restriction in rigid roles. When writing explicitly of the question of women's roles, Yonge becomes both more dogmatic and more dour.

All three of the brides, as has been said, chafe against the restrictions of marriage and the new family norms. However, their lives before marriage are also described in terms of restriction—of either over-protection or over-exertion. Cecil, an heiress and an only child, has been so carefully brought up as to have "no liberty, fewer indulgences and luxuries than many children, and never was permitted to be naughty" (16). For her, parental love has meant severe restriction. Her loveless marriage, which her husband enters into merely to provide a companion for his invalid mother, is merely a less palatable form of restriction, for as a wife she is aware that the curbs on her activities are not a matter of loving over-protection, and because she has no independent home, she has no sphere of power. Naturally she prefers the restrictions imposed on a darling daughter to the restrictions imposed on an unloved wife; outraged, she feels that she has come into "a rebellious world" (40). All the same Yonge presents her marriage as a movement not from liberty to constraint, but from constraint to constraint. Anne's life is presented in the same way. She, too, has never experienced freedom, and her strict upbringing has left her "poor little conscience" suffering in "terrible straits" (281) at any form of social pleasure. Even the cheerful Rosamond has experienced the burden of anxiety of the eldest child and most responsible member of "a large family with more rank and far more desires than means" (142).

The other unmarried women in the novel are also represented as perpetually and exceptionally constrained in their social relationships. For instance, an eventual fourth Charnock bride, Eleonora Vivian (married towards the end of the novel), is driven into depression and anxiety by the constraints of her position as younger sister to the powerful, devious and manipulative widow, Lady Tyrrell. She is "petrified by constant antagonism to such untruthfulness [in Lady Tyrrell] as where it cannot corrupt, almost always hardens those who come in contact with it" (103). She feels "like a French girl, always watched" (99). She responds to the "tacit persecution" (243) of her sister, who interferes both with her religious observances and her affection for Frank Charnock, with an exhausting "tacit resistance." Yonge emphasizes both Eleonora's obdurate strength and the intensity of her misery, which does not diminish until after her controlling sister's death. Women's lives—the lives of the unmarried as well as the married—are portrayed throughout this novel as involving frustration and constant restriction. The materfamilias, Mrs. Charnock Poynsett, for all her emotional and practical power over her sons and her estates, provides an emblem of women's lot in this novel, for she is totally paralysed and for most of the action confined to one room.

VII

Men are represented in *The Three Brides* as properly in the place of "lawful supremacy," while women as lawfully subordinated are also inevitably constricted. Yet women are represented here as holding another—potentially sinister—kind of power, the "natural supremacy" (153) of their place within the family and in their social interactions with men. Virtually all the women in this novel are strong and assertive individuals, but only the older women are free to exercise this power, and even their power is represented in various ways as being morally dubious. At the heart of this novel advocating the political powerlessness of women are two effectively powerful though frustrated women, Lady Tyrrell and Mrs. Charnock Poynsett. Mrs. Charnock Poynsett exercises control through her extensive property and her influence over her family; Lady Tyrrell exercises control through her extraordinary beauty, charm, and manipulative intelligence. The conflict between these two powerful women wrenches the lives of many of the other characters, and it is difficult to see it merely in terms of a conflict between vice and virtue (or the good mother and the bad mother), although Mrs. Charnock is represented as the beloved heart of the family and Lady Tyrrell as the wicked temptress. Both versions of active female power are represented as destructive.

Mrs. Charnock Poynsett is physically paralysed but socially and emotionally powerful. She is the owner of Compton Poynsett, the family seat, in her own right, inheriting it, that is, from her family of birth rather than her family of marriage, so that she has complete power over her home territory as well as unusual power over her five devoted sons. As a "beautiful young mother," she "had been the object of . . . adoration from the nursery upwards, so that she laughed at people who talked of the trouble and anxiety of rearing sons" (2). Although she is consistently described in positive terms, there is clearly some basis to Lady Tyrrell's jealous resentment of "her [Mrs. Charnock Poynsett's] power and [Raymond's] idolatry" (258). This mother-worship—they are often taken as "husband and wife rather than son and mother" (2), as the narrator says without any qualm—after all has helped destroy Raymond's relationship both with Lady Tyrrell, to whom he was once engaged, and with his wife; it also strains the loyalty of other characters. Thus although the narrator speaks of her in positive terms, the narrative shows the destructive effects of Mrs. Charnock Poynsett's power, especially in the life of her eldest son. Because of his mother's power over him Raymond can neither marry the woman he loves nor love the woman he marries. However, this maternal power is overtly presented as wholesome and appropriate. The narrative comment, though not the events themselves, makes it clear that though sexual power is dangerous and subversive, maternal power is safe. The emotional power of the widowed mother, after all, reinforces the authority of the hierarchy, which may well be subverted by the sexual.

Lady Tyrrell's power is certainly sexual rather than maternal: in her skillful manipulation of social situations through her own attractions and abilities, she resembles a demonized version of Bessie Keith in *The Clever Woman of the Family*.[11] "Far too clever, as well as too secure in her natural supremacy" to genuinely care very much for women's rights (153), she knows that her own power comes from her beauty, charm, and wit. She is treated in a quite different mode from any other character, being represented not just in terms of the conventions of realism but also through evocation of the legendary, the supernatural, the demonic: her original last name is Vivian, in allusion to the Arthurian enchantress whose story had quite recently (1859) been retold by Tennyson in strongly antifeminist terms; this allusion is underlined by the comments of the other characters and by the title of the chapter, "Vivienne," in which her deceptive art is most fully revealed. Her home is called Sirenwood, and her beauty is likened to that of a Florentine medal of the Medusa.[12] She controls completely the lives of her sister and her father, manipulates public opinion, and sabotages the already difficult marriage of Cecil and Raymond. The supernatural associations of her undoubted power are suggested further by the potent visions of each other that both she and Raymond, who were once in love, experience as they die of the fever, within twelve hours of each other. Women's power is represented in its most overtly threatening form through Lady Tyrrell. Yet, like the evil enchantress, the good mother wields power destructively within this narrative. Female power causes harm in *The Three Brides*.

VIII

Maternal power is presumably more acceptable not only because of its hierarchical implications but also because of its essentially private and domestic nature. The division between private and public life in this novel is total, so that any exercise of power beyond a woman's own home is necessarily suspect. The widowed mother as property owner and head of the family can legitimately exercise power within her own extensive private domain. Moreover, Mrs. Charnock Poynsett's power is legitimated not only by her family position but also by the completeness of her confinement to the private sphere caused by her paralysis. Women can be powerful as long as they are safely contained: Lady Tyrrell is threatening partly because the nature of her powers makes them virtually impossible to contain.

Because of this strong insistence on the private and domestic sphere in this novel women are represented as seriously jeopardizing their femininity and threatening the social fabric by public display, public speech, or joining in any activity that is understood as part of the public sphere. When Bessie Duncombe puts forward her idea of relief work at a public meeting, the Charnock family are disgusted not by her concern but by her unfeminine immodesty, her failure to prompt her husband to present her plan for her because "a woman spoils all the effect of her doings by putting herself out of her proper place" (56). A woman's proper place is essentially of course a private place: "the woman has much power of working usefully and gaining information, but the one thing that is not required of her is to come forward in public" (56). Public life is harmful to true femininity, a threat to gender identity: "the delicate edges of true womanhood ought not to be frayed off by exposure in public" (56).[13] The truly and uniquely feminine realm is the domestic: "the gain of an inferior power of man in public would be far from compensated by the loss in private of that which man can never supply" (56). Although many of Yonge's novels feature thoroughly domesticated men, as I have suggested in Chapter One and shall argue more fully below in the conclusion, this novel significantly is not among them. Again the moral superiority of women is used as an argument for curtailing their liberty. Similarly proper women should realise that it is an offence against gender to venture into the public realm of law, even in their own defence. Rosamond, who thinks that "any woman who is worth a sixpence had rather help her husband to shine than shine herself" (56), also believes that "nothing would induce a woman worth sixpence to take the law against her own husband" (160), even if that husband were beating her. In no circumstances does the truly feminine woman (a "woman worth sixpence") leave the private realm. Any form of public display is, as a defect in gender, not only socially but morally wrong.

Charlotte Yonge herself of course had a public name as a novelist successful throughout the English-speaking world. Her paradoxical position as a well-known woman advocating women's total avoidance of public life was hardly new: in the later years of the eighteenth century, as Jane Spencer notes, "women novelists were carving a public niche for themselves by recommending a private, domestic life for their heroines" (Spencer 20). In her portrayals of feminist activists, Yonge applies a gender criterion which affected the social thought of many of her contemporaries, and she exploits the power of this anxiety over women in public to rationalize the restriction of women to the domestic sphere.[14]

Similar anxieties about public life and public exposure inform literature throughout this period. Christina Rossetti's early and semi-autobiographical story *Maude*, for instance, represents an (admittedly misguided) young poet as feeling unworthy to receive holy communion because she is willfully sinful in "putting [her]self forward and displaying [her] verses" (25). Dinah Mulock Craik writes of "the instinctive something—call it reticence, modesty, shyness, what you will—that is inherent in every one of Eve's daughters" (37). This risk of being ungendered through the public gaze was obviously a difficulty for women in political life; even their supporters, such as Arthur Munby, expressed surprise that "there was nothing bold or 'unfeminine'" about the words and manners of the leaders of the suffrage movement when making speeches at their meetings (*FL* 120). Voting in itself was regarded as problematic for women because it was a public act. An opposing MP in 1867 argued that whereas a man would be ennobled by enfranchisement, a woman "would be almost debased or degraded by it. She would be in danger of losing those admirable attributes of her sex—namely, her gentleness, her affection, her domesticity" (Herstein 164). Supporters of women's suffrage expressed a similar anxiety about the fact that it was so "manifestly indecorous" for women "to attend the hustings or the polling booth" (Harman 357).

These difficulties affected some suffragists and many anti-suffragists. Elizabeth Garrett, on the one hand, wrote to Emily Davies when they were both reluctantly standing for the London School Board in 1870, "I dare say when it has to be done I can do it and it is no use asking for women to be taken into public work and yet to wish them to avoid publicity" (Hollis 74). On the other hand, Octavia Hill, the housing reformer, refused to sign an antisuffrage letter because signing a public document is a public act: "the very thing that makes me feel how fatal it would be for women to be drawn in to the public arena precludes my signing the letter and joining in what must be a political campaign" (Brian Harrison 112).

Such concerns about public decorum are evident in Yonge's other novels, but in *The Three Brides* they are foregrounded. Similarly, while elsewhere Yonge writes of women who are honourably active outside the domestic sphere, in this novel entirely devoted to considerations of gender she insists on women's close confinement to the private and the domestic world. Later she would express less rigid views, presenting with apparent approval in her final novel a Prize Day speech to women High School students that advocates that women compel attention by their achievements:

> The female population eagerly listened while she [Arthurine Arthuret, the speech-maker] painted in vivid colours the aim of education, in raising the status of women, and extending their spheres not only of influence in the occult manner which has hitherto been their way of working through others, but in an open manner, which compelled attention; and she dwelt on certain brilliant achievements of women, and of others which stood before them, and towards which their education, passing out of the old grooves, was preparing them to take their place among men, and temper their harshness and indifference to suffering with the laws of mercy and humanity, speaking with an authority and equality such as should ensure attention, not only in home and nursery whispering alone, but with open face asserting and claiming justice for the weakest. (*Modern Broods* 148)

The moral superiority of women, their natural alliance with "the laws of mercy and humanity," is still taken for granted, but it is no longer regarded as being so fragile that it will be shattered by public exposure.

IX

After *The Three Brides* and *Womankind* Yonge's work never again focused so strongly on the question of women's rights and status. In fact, after this point her work on the whole could be seen as regressing rather than progressing, in that she was certainly less responsive to public issues. Many of her later novels, written under financial constraint (see Introduction, note 17), take up characters from earlier works (or their children or grandchildren) and assume the form of the family chronicle that she had practiced with such success in *The Daisy Chain* and *The Pillars of the House*; it is likely that having lost much of her creative energy she was concerned to capitalize on her earlier successes. However, these late works show a continuing though less strenuous concern with the proper construction of gender, typically addressing the necessary subordination of young women to father, mother, aunt, or older sibling (see *Nuttie's Father, Two Sides of the Shield, Beechcroft at Rockstone, Modern Broods*).

One long short story from these years, "A Review of Nieces," published in *More Bye Words* (1890), demonstrates her on-going concern with issues of gender: the narrative functions as a parade of different modes of femininity, or a series of more or less successful definitions of femininity, showing the interplay of gender, religion, and class. In this story seven young women, all cousins, are unknowingly reviewed by their carefully named Aunt Charlotte, to see which is the most truly feminine of them, for the winner's reward is to be taken to Malta, where she will be "chief young lady in the place" (124) as the niece of General Fulford (the governor-general, presumably) and Aunt Charlotte, the sister who keeps house for him. The uncle's requirements are stringent: the chosen niece must be "well bred . . . enough to give a tone to the society of her contemporaries"; she must at least seem sexually unaware—"above all she must not flirt"; she must be pious—"she must have the only real spring of good breeding and be a thoroughly good, religious, unselfish, right-minded girl"; she must be educated and able—"there ought to be likewise intelligence and cultivation enough to profit by the opportunities that she will have"; and among other things she must also be tolerant—"you must have an eye likewise to good temper" (124). The aunt at least realises the impossibility of such a high feminine ideal but tells her brother that he will anyway "imagine all these charms in whatever good, ladylike, simple-hearted girl I pitch upon" (125).

The old-fashioned Aunt Charlotte is initially mistaken in her choice. Charlotte Yonge—the "Aunt Charlotte" of *Aunt Charlotte's Stories of English History for the Little Ones, Aunt Charlotte's Stories of Greek History for the Little Ones,* and half-a-dozen similar beginners' schoolbooks—clearly recognizes that in her sixties she was no longer as sharp in evaluating the characters of the young as she had once been.[15] The niece ultimately chosen is seen at first as being too unfeminine—"too much like a callow undergraduate" (necessarily then a male undergraduate) (128)—although Aunt Charlotte later sees that the "masculine dress"—the long coat and sailor hat—is in fact "quite ladylike" (131). However, another niece who is boyish for the sake of "defiance and coquetry" (131) is out of the question, as are the two nieces who, though devoutly religious, are ill-dressed and too provincial in their manners. A scholarly niece, "always whipping out a microscope and lecturing upon protoplasms," who is also devoted to the cause of "the emancipation of women" (149), is automatically unacceptable to her uncle: "the learned young lady is out of the question" (183). So is the prettiest niece, who is flirtatious. The ingratiatingly sweet niece originally favoured by the aunt turns out to be "a horrid little treacherous puss."

The niece finally chosen is well-mannered and considerate (she is polite to a poor invalid); she is self-sacrificing (she gives her dress allowance to the needy); she is clear-headed (she doesn't panic during a fire-scare); she is well-educated (she identifies allusions to Dante in a painting). The point of this story depends entirely on an assessment of the ideal of femininity, and the chosen niece is all the more ideal in her femininity for being hardly noticed at first—she has the "unselfish yielding spirit" (177) which Yonge consistently praises in her work as an essential of femininity. She is called Avice, too, probably in a typical Yongean allusion to the phrase *rara avis*—this ideal of young ladyhood is a rare bird indeed. In the last decade of her career, Yonge's interest in the nature of femininity continues to give form to her writing—the entire plot of this story depends on gender codes.

This late story shows Yonge recognizing the changes in the lives and behaviour of young women, as she does all the way through the last part of her long career, in the twenty-five years after *The Three Brides*. However, after this point she feels that she is no longer part of the current of events: "I am getting too old to write of the swing of modern life; I don't see enough of it," she wrote in 1885, and she told Ethel Romanes that she "could not feel in sympathy with much of these newer phases of thought" (Romanes 185, 190). Never again does she give such a sharp response to contemporary events and to the changes in the women's movement.

In Yonge's earlier novels, while consistently celebrating the domestic, she also valorizes social utility for men and women alike, which usually implies some kind of liberty: Ethel May of *The Daisy Chain* is useful to her domestic circle but probably even more effective in her social work at Cocksmoor, and Rachel, Ermine, and Alison in *The Clever Woman of the Family* are all active and useful women, at least at certain stages of their careers. All the same, an element of frustration is built into their narratives: Ethel's academic and literary ambitions are frustrated through her own choice, and she avoids for her father's sake a man to whom she is strongly attracted; Rachel's feminist ambitions are frustrated through her gullibility; Ermine is immobilized, and Alison has renounced the man she once wanted to marry—this renunciation is for the sake of her sister, and not, as in Ethel's case, her father. While Yonge gradually becomes increasingly focused on material that is related to the public discussion of women's issues, she consistently equates femininity with some kind of frustration, some kind of curb.

A high degree of frustration seems a necessary part of the development of any of Yonge's more fully-treated women characters. In *The Three Brides*, however, frustration is foregrounded to an unprecedented extent, and though usefulness is valued, all the women in this novel are finally left in a narrow domestic sphere. Yonge responds to a call for political freedom by pointing firmly to social and emotional chains.

97

EPILOGUE

"The Trivial Round, the Common Task": Gender and the Domestic Novel

In the preceding chapters Yonge's fascination with codes of gender has been examined through selected novels and situated in the changing context of the discourse of the nineteenth-century women's movement. Yonge's fiction is shown as becoming increasingly engaged with the current debates about women. In *The Daisy Chain*, a comparatively early novel, Yonge's treatment of educational trends is very much at arm's length: her critique of the changes in women's education—its increasing institutionalization and potential secularization—works entirely by implication. *The Clever Woman of the Family*, almost ten years later, is far more directly and explicitly involved with issues of women and work, as Yonge presents an energetic, frustrated, and misguided young woman, while quietly satirizing the activities of contemporary feminist sympathizers. Still later, *The Three Brides* tackles political issues generally but directly, through open debate and portrayals of women activists, while women's legal concerns are dealt with indirectly by foregrounding the subject of hierarchy within marriage. The nature of Yonge's engagement with the "woman question" develops and changes, although her preoccupation with ideas of gender and the feminine role persists.

One unsurprising constant throughout her work is the valorizing of the domestic and the predictable connection between femininity and the domestic. Despite this reiterated concern, Yonge is not especially interested in the notion of separate spheres for men and women, their segregation into the private or the public; the conventional distaste she expresses for the notion of women invading the public realm seems largely an expression of a genuine distaste for the public realm as such, as dangerous both physically and spiritually. Anne Mellor points out that earlier in the century some women writers "rejected the public sphere altogether as irredeemably brutal, corrupt, and self-destructive" (83). Yonge follows this feminine tradition. Like her feminist contemporaries —Josephine Butler writes of home as "the nursery of all virtues, the fountainhead of all the affections, and the main source of the strength of our nation" (xxv)—she valorizes domestic values, seeing the home as the arena of moral and religious engagement.

Because of this view of the public and the private, Yonge's male characters as well as her heroines are frequently understood in relation to domestic values; they are feminized at least to the extent that they are domesticated.[1] The discussion of The *Daisy Chain* and *The Trial* in Chapter One suggested that Dr. May is essentially a domestic character, the emotional centre of his family, while Tom May's story is one of conversion from public and professional ambitions to private and domestic aims; that discussion also outlined some of the implications of seeing the domestic as an essential moral arena for women and men alike. Here my investigation of Yonge's gender ideology moves finally to the question of masculinity and the domestic, using as examples the best-seller *The Heir of Redclyffe* (1853) and *The Pillars of the House* (1873-74), both of which have feminized heroes.[2] In these novels, as in the novels discussed above, the discourse of gender changes according to its historical and generic context; in these concluding pages, I explore the interaction of religion, gender, and class in relation not to the changing discourse of the woman question but to generic considerations. *The Heir of Redclyffe* shows Yonge's domestic vision embracing and engulfing the masculine through a fusion of "realist" domestic novel and romance, as Sir Guy Morville of Redclyffe becomes the domesticated hero of romance. *The Pillars of the House*, by contrast a family chronicle after the model of *The Daisy Chain*, exploits a less adulterated realist vein to foreground in a different way the details of the mundane and the commonplace as part of Christian moral life.

Inevitably at a period when the identification between self-sacrifice and femininity was especially strong, the sacrifice of Christ was often seen in feminine terms.[3] Yonge forcibly expresses her distaste for the idea of a feminized Christ:

> Shame on those who have lowered the idea of religion by such teaching [that spiritual gifts are essentially feminine]. Nay, they have even read the Gospels so as to fancy that the holiness of Him Who was Perfect God as well as Perfect Man was of feminine type. They do not see the might of Him Who stood alone . . . The intense calmness and absence of all violence have perhaps been some excuse for those who have missed the impression of undaunted unflinching resolution, and stern indignation against evil; but it is a miserable error, a sin in itself because it is derogatory to the honour of the Lord Who bought us, and false when it alienates us from His example as if not meant for men as much as for women. (*Womankind* 234)

Predictably Yonge identifies the "might," the "undaunted, unflinching resolution," and the "stern indignation" that she sees in the gospels as masculine, while the "calmness and absence of violence" are regarded as possible indications of femininity. Yet undeniably Yonge's Christian heroes share the domestic values of the women of her novels and are judged by their share of qualities normally connected with the feminine, such as nurturing, self-sacrifice, gentleness, and sympathy. Moreover Yonge's affirmation of the domestic and, more specifically, the domestic novel in its foregrounding of detail and restriction also valorizes the feminine.

I

Dickens with a natural pique reported in *Household Words* the case of a young woman who refused to read any novel other than *The Heir of Redclyffe*. As soon as she reached the ending, she started right over again with Chapter One (2.620). This novel, indeed, exerts the double fascination of romance and domestic fiction; as Sandbach-Dahlstrom shows, "the story of Sir Guy Morville . . . is a Romance fable which takes place in a recognizable social milieu" (29).[4] Yonge acknowledged wryly her youthful penchant for romantic clichés when commenting late in life on another early book, *Scenes and Characters*: "that in a youthful composition there should be a cavalier ancestry, a family much given to dying of consumption, and a young marquess cousin, is, perhaps, inevitable" (*TSS* vii). *The Heir of Redclyffe* partly liberates itself from romantic cliché: it represents the absorption of the heroic into the domestic, in the christianizing, feminizing, and domesticating of "a knight of the Round Table, in name and nature" (*Heir* 395-96), an absorption typical of domestic fiction. Nancy Armstrong, writing of *Pride and Prejudice*, describes the domestic novel as showing the male, powerful in the public and political domain, as drawn into the site of feminine power, the domestic and emotional sphere (51). As I have suggested, this is the case with Tom May in *The Trial*. In *The Heir of Redclyffe* this typical domestic narrative of gender relationships is especially compelling because the hero is strongly identified with a variety of traditions of male power, while his absorption into the female sphere is clearly marked both as spiritual salvation and as happy homecoming. Moreover, the novel as a whole represents a kind of moral interaction between the domestic and the heroic, and establishes both novel and heroic romance as playing an essential role in moral education. Ultimately the domestic prevails: domestic values provide a resolution for heroic conflicts, and the home itself becomes the site of exploits worthy of Christian heroes.

100

Sir Guy Morville of Redclyffe has all the appropriate fictional trappings of male power—land, great wealth, an Oxford education, a title, intellect, exceptional physical energy, and a prospective political career. He is a romantic figure as the last of an ancient and historic family: the Morvilles are presented as descendants of one of Thomas à Becket's assassins, and Guy's "ancient name and long ancestry" are said to cause even his cousin, rival, and heir, Philip Morville, "to look up to him with a feudal feeling as head of the family" (97). Guy is, moreover, the inheritor of a vast, ruinous, and gloomy mansion, "more like a scene in a Romance than anything real," again according to the envious Philip (7). In action, as well as in situation, Guy is recognizable as the chivalric hero, for his repeated exploits as a life-saver establish him as a worthy hero of romance: he saves the lives of the entire crew of a storm-wrecked ship; he saves his young wife, Amy, by dragging her back as she slips from an Alpine precipice; and, at the turning point of the novel, he saves his enemy, Philip, by nursing him through a severe fever, thus risking and ultimately sacrificing his own life. Guy is also explicitly a Christian hero, saving souls as well as bodies: with her salvation in view (219), he pays for the education of a poor little cousin who is quite untaught in religious matters and leaves money in his will to endow a teaching and nursing sisterhood. He is in fact Christ-like, and the repentant Philip eventually comes to suggest for Guy's epitaph words applied to Christ: "greater love has no man than this, that he lay down his life for his friend" (428; John 15:3). As his cousins say, he is "a hero model" (518), the perfect Christian gentleman, and a nineteenth-century martyr.

Guy's family history is also heroic, being explicitly associated with two romantic tropes, the feud and the curse. His difficult relationship with Philip is repeatedly described in terms of the feuds of romance: "there is a deadly feud between the two branches of the house of Morville" (13), and the narrative as a whole implies that this feud can be resolved only by the saving and the sacrifice of a life (76, 338)—Guy's life for Philip's, in the event. Guy also speaks of himself as under a family curse (61), identifying himself with De La Motte Fouqué's Sintram, who like Guy is apparently doomed as a member of a sinful family. "Crime and bloodshed had been the portion of each—each has added weight and darkness to the doom he has handed on," says Guy of his family history ever since the Archbishop's murder. However, both feud narrative and curse narrative are eventually resolved through the domestic, through Guy's "coming home" to the house of his guardian, Mr. Edmonstone, whose wife is by birth one of the rival Morville branch. Guy eventually marries their daughter, Amy, establishes a filial relationship with her parents and a fraternal relationship with her brother and sisters (Charles, Laura, and Charlotte), thus reconciling the two branches of the family. Through his influence on the family and posthumously on Philip, he finally brings a deeper tranquillity to the Edmonstones' domestic life. In *The Three Brides* Yonge describes marriage explicitly and dogmatically in terms of women merging into the families of their husbands; here in the earlier novel the narrative shows Guy's marriage as of spiritual value partly because it involves his membership in Amy's family, as the Byronic hero comes home.[5]

The Edmonstones' home is represented as a place of spiritual refreshment: it is carefully named "Hollywell." From the first words of the novel, a protracted description of its drawing room—"one of the favoured apartments, where a peculiar air of home seems to reside" (1)—home is emphasized as a central value, and Hollywell functions as the embodiment of home. For both Guy and Philip, it is a substitute for their own deserted homes, the homes that will obsess both of them in delirium when they are seriously ill with the fever. The moral health of both men is evaluated on the basis of their relationship to Hollywell, as their adopted home and the home of Amy and Laura, the sisters they love.

Guy's religious virtues are made apparent by his acceptance of domestic values, by his chivalrous devotion not only to his sweetheart, Amy, but to her home and to her entire family. He is especially attached to her mother. Before Guy's engagement to Amy, Charles speaks of Mrs. Edmonstone as Guy's "first and only love" (135), and when he is dying Guy tells Amy that it was her likeness to her mother "that first taught me to love you" (411). Mrs. Edmonstone in turn is equally emphatic in claiming their relationship: after the wedding she tells Guy, "I little thought how truly and how gladly I should be able to call you my son" (340). Guy constantly reiterates his new sense of family, repeatedly speaking of and writing to the younger Edmonstones as "my brother and sisters." His happiness after Amy accepts his proposal of marriage is described in these terms:

> Guy . . . isolated and lonely as he stood in life, with his fear and mistrust of himself, was now not only allowed to love and assured beyond his hopes that Amy returned his affection, but found himself thus welcomed by the mother, and gathered into the family where his warm feelings had taken up their abode, while he believed himself regarded only as a guest and stranger.
>
> (167)

By contrast, Philip's insistence on his own social, moral, and intellectual superiority and on the preeminence of his own emotional claims subverts the family network. Yonge presents the concealment of the attachment between Laura and Philip as a serious offence, not because of any imagined impropriety, but rather because it represents treachery to Laura's parents and her home — her mother reproaches her, "you forget that you are a daughter" (393). Laura's fault is not that she regards herself as independent but that she acts as a possession of Philip rather than of her parents. The novel's resolution is not Guy's happy marriage to Amy, nor his heroic death (which occurs more than a hundred pages before the end of the novel), but the final justification of his code of domestic Christianity, when Philip and Laura both eventually accept their obligations to the parental home, and the widowed Amy and her child are restored to Hollywell: "it is a blessing that my own dear home can open to take in me and baby," she says (523).

Like Rochester and St. John Rivers in *Jane Eyre*, first published six years before *The Heir of Redclyffe* in 1847, Guy and Philip represent two different modes of masculinity, and the contrast between them is part of the motive for the novel, though Yonge describes it in religious terms rather than in terms of gender: "in the May of 1850 a friend . . . told me there were two characters she wanted to see brought out in a story — namely the essentially contrite [Guy] and the self-satisfied [Philip]" (Romanes 63). The self-satisfied Philip, indeed, strongly resembles St. John; he, too, is exceptionally tall, handsome, brilliant, imposing, pious, controlled, controlling, and complacent. Like Brontë in this respect if no other, Yonge rejects this aggressive mode of religious masculinity for the less conventionally masculine warmth and liveliness of Guy. Both novels, that is, reject an authoritarian patriarchal male figure in favour of a more emotional version of masculinity, a masculine that is essentially interdependent with the feminine, though Yonge's hero is, of course, not so much the erotic male as the domestic male. Rochester and Jane provide a world for each other; Guy becomes absorbed into Amy's domestic world. Meanwhile Philip, the dominant male, has to learn humility through illness, contrition, and his complete dependence on the kindness, support, and forgiveness of Amy, whom he has dismissed for most of the novel as "silly little Amy," in the assumption that her character has "no bones" (10).[6]

Yonge's work represents a kind of apotheosis of the domestic novel, both in the explicit claims made for the important role played by novels and romances in moral education, and in that she consistently represents domesticity as the sphere for moral action, the apparently insignificant becoming the morally essential.[7] Throughout *The Heir of Redclyffe* family interactions and social life — the ball, the dinner party, the morning visit—are imagined in terms of spiritual as well as social values and evaluated as moral obligations, enabling those among Yonge's readers who were confined to the domestic realm to re-imagine their own existence in larger terms. The apparently petty details of everyday speech and action, which Keble describes as "the trivial round, the common task" (*CY* 4), are invested with religious and moral importance. For instance, Guy is distressed when his passing comment on a woman who had tried one cigar is exaggerated by Charles into an amusing piece of gossip about how she has "a regular order for [cigars from] Havannah"; the narrative places Guy's linguistic precision not as "straining at gnats" (52) as Charles claims, but as a concern for exact truth and justice over the slightest detail.

This insistence on the spiritual importance of the trivial is understood in religious terms. "Trifles" are defined (by means of a parlour game) thus: "Little things / On little wings / Bear little souls to Heaven" (35). Here Yonge writes both as domestic novelist and as Tractarian. Hurrell Froude's *Remains* (1838), one of the documents that first made Tractarianism controversial, notoriously shows its author as guilt-ridden over scruples of conscience and minutiae of thought and behaviour: as his friend Newman says, "he embraced the principle of penance and mortification" (596). Sir Guy's delicately-tuned conscience and exaggerated penance have frequently been considered in the light of Froude's *Remains*.[8] Yonge herself invokes the parallel, for early in her work on this novel, she was delighted by her mother's response to a description of Sir Guy: "when she heard him described she said 'Like Mr. Hurrell Froude' which," Yonge says with satisfaction, "I hope is a sign that I have got the right sow by the ear" (Coleridge 170). Guy's spiritual strength is expressed in terms of infinite care over the details of the moral life and the ceaseless apportioning of guilt. This approach to the spiritual life could lead a man like Keble to feel such unrealistic "self-blame" at "every lapse in his parish" (*JKP* 124), that he began to consider resigning because "all his best efforts had failed to raise the people to his own standard of religion" (*JKP* 142), as Yonge herself says. *The Heir of Redclyffe* enables Yonge, as Keble's devoted pupil, to demonstrate this refinement of conscience in a quasi-heroic action.

II

Twenty years after the great success of *The Heir of Redclyffe*, in *The Pillars of the House*, Yonge largely, though not entirely, abandons the romance, adhering far more closely to domestic realism in a novel that again valorizes the details of social interaction partly through its use of the domestic male.[9] Although Yonge here reverts to the family chronicle, the later novel is not merely a variant on *The Daisy Chain*, with which it has several (May family) characters in common. It differs radically from the earlier novel, simply by moving down the social—or at least the pecuniary—ladder, and thus foregrounding a different range of details with different implications. For the Underwood family "the trivial round, the common task" are indeed trivial and common in ways that they cannot be for Sir Guy, the wealthy baronet, or for the Mays, the carefully educated and protected family of a prosperous physician. The thirteen young Underwoods, orphaned and left with only a tiny income when the eldest of them is only sixteen years old and the youngest newly born,[10] have to deal with such unheroic matters as frayed shirt-cuffs, boot-blacking, threadbare carpets, and the price of eggs. While in *The Heir of Redclyffe* Yonge celebrates the domestic novel by absorbing romance elements into the elements of domestic fiction, here she celebrates the domestic novel by foregrounding the details of everyday domestic survival. Moral weight is invested in all the essential practical minutiae of household management as well as in the social interactions that are so significant in the earlier novel. As with *Robinson Crusoe* the appeal of *The Pillars of the House* depends largely on a close account of economic survival, but while Defoe is concerned with the survival of the isolated individual, Yonge's focus is economic survival as a family unit, so that the family stays together, struggles together, and eventually succeeds together—a cosier and more domestic version of the bourgeois myth.

In their struggle with poverty the eldest Underwood brother and sister, Felix and Wilmet, take on the gender roles of the Puritan family as described by Armstrong (110); in Yonge's terms (when she is describing the beliefs of a worthy but narrow-minded provincial lady), "the dignified and lady-like mission of the well-born woman [is] to be not the bread-winner [like the man], but the preserver and steward of the household" (*MB* 1.177). Their survival as a family depends both on the ability of the brother to bring home the money and more especially on the power of the sister to lay out the income. In a curious variant, however, while the power of the feminine is acknowledged in the household—Wilmet (like Ethel May before her) is recognized as the effective family authority, exacting unquestioning obedience—the male becomes the emotional centre of the household: the younger siblings invariably turn to Felix for support and sympathy. Here as elsewhere in Yonge, while the female is the source of energy, the male is the source of feeling and thus of domestic security. Wilmet herself confides in Felix when she falls in love,

105

feeling he "took the place of both parents—aye, and of sister, too" (1.384); Angela tells him of her secret desire to join a sisterhood; Edgar actually reproaches Felix for being more like a sister than a brother in his concern for Edgar's spiritual well-being (1.229); all his dozen siblings, in fact, accept him as their strongest family tie, their emotional as well as their legal next-of-kin. For Felix himself, his family home is what matters to him "more than aught save the home beyond" (2.505). Felix is so strongly associated with the home that, as Sandbach-Dahlstrom shows, after his death the family disperses, moving away from the ancestral home (to which they have been restored) towards "the claims of the modern world" (Sandbach-Dahlstrom 93).

In *The Pillars of the House* Yonge deals again as she had done in *The Trial* with the problems of a young family without parents and their efforts to maintain family unity and security. In *The Trial*, when the eldest brother is forced into the paternal role, his authoritarian attitude leads to family breakdown, violence, and an accusation of murder. Felix Underwood (of *The Pillars of the House*) is explicitly contrasted with Henry Ward (of *The Trial*) in this regard, when Dr. May, a character in both novels, compares the different fates of the two orphaned families. In the later novel the self-sacrifice and scrupulously loving parental care of the guardian brother is what binds the family together. He takes on the parental role as nurturer rather than as authority, acting maternally rather than paternally. Again, as with Guy and Philip in *The Heir of Redclyffe*, a conventional view of male power is subverted by the preference given to the domestic male.

The continuing family stability of the Underwoods depends on the sacrifice of not just one brother, but two. The fifth brother, Lance, as well as the eldest brother, Felix, must give up social position and ambition for the sake of the family business and the support of their numerous brothers and sisters. When Lance goes into the family business—into "trade" as bookseller, publisher, and editor—like Felix he sacrifices social caste for the sake of the family's survival as an economic and social unit; as a tradesman he is disqualified from membership in the gentry. He also sacrifices his exceptional talent as a musician, a talent that is described in terms which suggest that he might have become a great singer, a violinist, a pianist, or a composer (Yonge was not musical). The self-abnegation of both Felix and Lance may well be a reflection of Keble's own renunciation of his brilliant Oxford career and literary fame for the sake of a small parish and the care of his ailing father.[11] Throughout the novel Lance especially is presented as spontaneously self-denying: he sells his precious violin to get a little brother out of debt, and makes himself seriously ill with sunstroke helping a school fellow. He is not concerned with his male dignity any more than with his rights: he cheerfully runs errands to the local grocery, helps Wilmet cook (252), and washes, irons and mends his own clothes on occasion.

The brothers' sacrifice is presented as an anti-romantic version of the heroic, a domestic heroism: the "unconventional" (2.359) Gertrude, youngest of the May family, comments when she learns the Underwood family history, "whenever I think of a hero I shall think of Mr. Under- wood. . . . To turn tradesman for the sake of one's brothers and sisters, that I do call heroic" (1.373). The narrative makes this view of the emotional toll of renouncing class and status convincing: both brothers, and especially the sociable Lance, suffer from their precarious social position. Eventually the younger "hero," Lance, is rewarded for his sacrifices by the hand of Gertrude.

III

Yonge's treatment of the masculine in both her most concentratedly domestic novel—*The Pillars of the House*—and in her domestic romance —*The Heir of Redclyffe*—shows an essentially domesticated vision of the heroic male, as self-sacrificing and devoted to the family, as willing to suffer loss of dignity, prestige and caste, as nurturing and affectionate. The more conventionally patriarchal male in her novels is frequently shown to be in need of correction, of softening, of acknowledging his own dependence; in need, in fact, in Yonge's terms, of conversion.[12] Her interest in the feminine engages her in a changing dialogue with the various currents in the women's movements of the nineteenth century, but her preoccupation with the family and with a domesticated Chris- tianity leads her throughout her career to feminize her heroes, to bring them into the moral centre, the middle-class English home.

Yonge's domestic fiction enables her as the devoted pupil of John Keble to demonstrate Keble's typical lines quoted earlier:

> The trivial round, the common task
> Will furnish all we ought to ask:
> Room to deny ourselves—a road
> To bring us daily nearer God.
> *(CY 4)*[13]

She elaborates in fiction the values associated with Keble's Tractarianism through his life, his prose writings, and the poems of *The Christian Year* and the *Lyra Innocentium*, the values of self-denial transforming "Life's dullest, dreariest walk" (*CY* 2) into a spiritual journey.

Yonge's religious writing differs from the work of many of her female contemporaries and predecessors in that she eschewed the feminine prophetic voice about which Christine Krueger has written so convincingly. Nor could her work be included among the "oracular novels" that George Eliot connects with High Church teaching (Eliot 313), for her heroines are by no means uniformly beautiful, good, and witty in accordance with Eliot's satirical description—Amy is much less pretty and clever than Laura, Ethel is known as the plain May sister, and Rachel is accustomed to think of her appearance as "repellently practical and intellectual" (*CWF* 113-14). Yonge connects the religious life not with emotion and with exhortation; on the contrary she insists on the religious reserve associated with Tractarianism, a "wholesome reserve which shrinks from obtruding itself or flaunting its badges either for praise or blame" (*Womankind* 217). She sees religion in moral terms, as action rather than emotion; when a character becomes disillusioned with the religious life she is sternly asked "You tried to feel; what did you try to do?" (*Castle Builders* 290). "Doing" is seen not as the unique melodramatic gesture but as the unremarkable daily activity.

Such a concept of the religious life offers a kind of vindication to the domestic novelist, who is inevitably concerned with the quotidian and the habitual. Yonge writes of her fiction in the preface to one of her earliest novels, *The Two Guardians*, that

> throughout these tales the plan has been to present a picture of ordinary life with its small daily events, its pleasures and its trials, so as to draw out its capabilities of being turned to the best account. Great events, such as befall only a few, are thus excluded and in the hope of helping to present a clue, by example, to the perplexities of daily life, the incidents, which render a story exciting, have been sacrificed. (iii)[14]

Yonge's later novels certainly offer plenty of "great events," such as shipwrecks (*The Heir of Redclyffe, The Daisy Chain*), daring rescues from desperate revolutionaries (*Dynevor Terrace*), murder (*The Trial*), fires (*The Three Brides, The Pillars of the House, Heartsease*), war (*The Young Stepmother*), robberies with attempted murder (*Hopes and Fears*), drownings (*The Castle Builders, The Pillars of the House*) and so on. Yet they foreground not these events, which on the whole merely move along the plots, but the "small daily events," so much so that a contemporary reviewer complained of Yonge's work that "you have all the small life as well as the eventful; you sit down to nearly every breakfast, you are admitted every day to almost every room."[15]

This exaggeration is based on an accurate perception of a quality that is demonstrably present in Yonge's novels, a sense of close proximity to the ongoing life of households—to the domestic pulse. As Mermin says, "in Yonge's books religion endows seemingly insignificant actions with crucial—literally, life and death—importance. . . . For Yonge, religion justifies the novelist's vocation by affirming the importance of uneventful, restricted lives" (*Godiva's Ride* 110). Helen, one of Yonge's plain and humdrum saints (in *Heartsease*, which is contemporary with *The Daisy Chain* and *The Heir of Redclyffe*), writes thus of the minutiae of the moral life, affirming the importance of her own drearily restricted existence and quoting in passing the words of Keble's hymn:

> That dressmaker must have been a happy woman who never took home her work without praying that it might fit. I always liked that story particularly, as it shows how the practical life in the most trivial round can be thus united with thus casting all our care upon Him—the being busy in our own station with choosing the good part. (134)

The spiritual significance of the practical, and of the apparently trivial and the minute, validates domestic fiction; it also validates the traditionally feminine, because of the traditional cultural association between the feminine and the particular, which, according to Naomi Schor, "spans not only cultures but centuries, extending from antiquity to the present day" (17). Yonge's version of Tractarianism ennobles and dramatizes the domestic details inevitably preoccupying many of her middle-class women readers throughout the second half of the nineteenth century; it re-presents their lives to them.

NOTES

[1] For instance she uses it as the epigraph to chapter ten of Part Two of *The Daisy Chain* (441), describes the pious and patriotic Irishman, Ulick O'More, by the same phrase in *The Young Stepmother* (259), and begins her chapter on "Home" in *Womankind* with these words: "The Altar and the hearth! Well may they be coupled together and well does Wordsworth in his 'Lark' describe the faithful heart as 'True to the kindred points of Heaven and Home!'" (264).

[2] Two expressions are used with conscious anachronism throughout this work for convenience, namely "middle-class" and "feminist." Yonge would have described herself not as middle-class but as the daughter of a member of the landed gentry. The mid-Victorians commonly identified the middle class with certain occupational groups. Thus, for example, in 1865 *The Guardian* refers to the middle class as made up principally of farmers, retail dealers, and clerks (Heeney, *Mission* 6). Class and occupation are associated with the school-leaving age of the sons of the family: "middle-class boys are boys whose general education ends between their fourteenth and their nineteenth years of age" (Heeney, *Mission* 9). As Rendall points out the English word "feminism" was not in use at this period; the French word "feminisme" was coined and used exclusively by the Utopian socialist, Charles Fourier, but recent historians have found the word an essential tool for analysis (Rendall 1). Levine further argues that the use of the term is not anachronistic (*VFU* 14).

[3] As late as 1886 in a survey of what girls read she comes third in popularity, tied with Kingsley, after Dickens and Scott, but ahead of Shakespeare and Brontë (Flint, *Woman Reader* 158). Her female readership seems to have lasted longer than her male readership, after the overwhelming general popularity of *The Heir of Redclyffe* in the 1850s, but all the same she was mobbed by an enthusiastic crowd of undergraduates and young dons on a visit to Cambridge in the early 1870s (Mare and Percival 218).

[4] "It is only as a daughter of the Church that woman can have her place or be satisfied as to her vocation" (*Womankind* 20).

[5] See Chapter Two on the relationship between *Emma* and *The Clever Woman of the Family*. *Scenes and Characters* appears to re-use elements of *Sense and Sensibility*, and *The Trial* of *Pride and Prejudice*.

[6] Helsinger, Sheets, and Veeder provide a good introduction to this subject.

[7] The subtitle of Georgina Battiscombe's Yonge biography is "the story of an uneventful life."

8 For instance a good son thinks it appropriate to give up a vocation as a clergyman because his father wants him to be a soldier (*The Castle Builders*); a sensible adult woman thinks it appropriate to refuse to marry the excellent man she loves and to go to Peru to join her debauched and prejudiced father, at his whim (*Dynevor Terrace*). Most of Yonge's novels include similar examples.

9 Similar December-May marriages appear in many novels. Lucilla in *Hopes and Fears* marries Mr. Prendergast who has loved her ever since she was a tiny child and he her father's curate. Bessie Keith (of *The Clever Woman in the Family*) in her early twenties marries a Scottish laird in his late fifties. In *Nuttie's Father* both Nuttie and her mother marry men old enough to be their fathers. Helen in "Last Heartsease Leaves" marries a man who is at least in his early twenties when she is born; many more examples can be found.

10 At fifteen she had published *Le Chateau de Melville*, a little book of the French stories written for her tutor, in order to raise some money for church-building.

11 The facsimile of a letter dated 1895 (Mare and Percival 208) shows this gossip in relation to *The Long Vacation*.

12 The successful writer in question, Bessie Merrifield, is represented as feeling compunction at having written a book about the sufferings of an orphan girl brought up by an aunt which causes one of its young readers great misery when she has to live with her aunt. It is possible that Yonge is thinking here of her own *Countess Kate*, which shows the difficulties of a wild little girl taken in by aristocratic relations; or she may merely be following the tradition in women's writing of satirizing women readers as likely to read fiction as a guide to life—the tradition of *Northanger Abbey*, or Charlotte Lennox's *Female Quixote*.

13 The "Langley" series is intended for Sunday School children, that is, children of lower social status than Yonge's; novels like *Countess Kate* and *The Stokesley Secret* are intended for children of her own class.

14 Other biographies are those of the late Prince Consort and Hannah More. The other works referred to are her *History of Christian Names*, *An Old Woman's Outlook in a Hampshire Village*, and *John Keble's Parishes*.

15 Showalter lists Jewsbury, Adeline Sergeant, Minna Featherstonehaugh, Gertrude Mayer, Lady Dorchester, and Mrs. G. W. Godfrey as women readers for Bentley's (*Literature* 157).

16 Levine refers to Jihaang Park's analysis of women included in biographical compendia of the period, which shows that in the 1862 edition of *Men of the Time* writers, excluding journalists but including actresses and musicians, constituted 78 per cent of the female entries (*FL* 5).

17 Although for much of her professional life her profits went to charity—the profits of *The Heir of Redclyffe* and *The Daisy Chain* were used to support missionary work in Melanesia (Dennis 32)—she still understood the importance of the economic motive: "Literature, like other avocations open to women, is all the worse for those really dependent on it, because they are undersold by those to whom remuneration is unimportant, and this out of ignorance and desire to gain a hearing. Therefore, it is right to insist on a fair price, and not to close in haste with any offer

for less" ("Authorship," *Chaplet* 190). After 1876 her earning capacity was needed to help support her brother's family when he lost money speculating in a coal mining business (Dennis 33; Foster 340); Yonge decided to sell her copyrights (Tuchman 165) and apparently attempted to step up her diminishing profits.

[18] Newman, for instance, writes of his beliefs during the Tractarian period of his religious life that he criticized one of Thomas Arnold's pieces of biblical interpretation in this way: "Arnold answers for the interpretation, but who is to answer for Arnold?" (603).

[19] The Contagious Diseases Acts "gave police in certain military towns the power to require regular internal examination for syphilis of any woman suspected of being a prostitute, and to place her in a 'Lock' hospital until she was pronounced cured" (Brown 213). As any woman could be stopped by the police, the acts threatened working women in general as well as prostitutes in particular. See Walkowitz for further discussion.

[20] Butler deliberately associates feminists with domestic happiness: "it is precisely this abundance of [domestic] blessing bestowed on them that urges them to care for the less happy" (xxv).

[21] Yonge comments on Keble's editing of her work, "in general the purport of his remarks was to guard to the utmost both delicacy and reverence" (Battiscombe, *Yonge* 72). For the sake of the plot of *The Heir of Redclyffe*, however, the fact that "poor Amy is to be confined in the spring" has to be made known (423).

[22] For instance, Amy in *The Heir of Redclyffe*, Margaret May in *The Daisy Chain*, Clara Frost in *Dynevor Terrace*, Gertrude May in *The Pillars of the House*, and Sydney in *Magnum Bonum*.

[23] Therefore one feminist campaign of which there is not even a whisper in Yonge's work is the campaign over the Contagious Diseases Acts. Macmillan, Yonge's publisher, also published a collection of essays edited by Josephine Butler in 1869, *Women's Work and Women's Culture*. This omits any direct discussion of the subject, but Butler felt it essential to indicate her sympathies: "the subject was thought too painful an one to be specially treated in a volume for general reading; therefore I think it more needful to assert that these our fellow-women are not forgotten by us; on the contrary we continually feel . . . the wholesale destruction that goes on from year to year among women; destruction of bodies, of consciences, of souls" (xx).

[24] Cobbe refers to woman being seen variously as domestic, social, and political; as Goddess, Doll, the Angel in the House, or a Drudge; as one who has a "Mission," a "Sphere," a "Kingdom" (1).

[25] Thompson contrasts this novel with its near-contemporary, *Wuthering Heights*, which Anne Mellor examines in *Romanticism and Gender* as a piece of masculine romanticism.

[26] This is necessarily a simplification of Barbara Leigh Smith Bodichon's political career, which also included serious work on the Married Women's Property question; after about 1870 she directed her efforts to helping found Girton College, Cambridge. My comments on Bodichon are indebted to Sheila Herstein's account of her career.

[1] There are two brief visits to London, in chapters eighteen and twenty.

[2] The first of two parts was published in *The Monthly Packet* in 1853-55; the whole novel appeared in book form in 1856.

[3] Regina M. Janes's article on the reception of *A Vindication* discusses both its early success and the silencing caused by popular fear of causes associated with revolution and by the scandal following Godwin's publication in 1798 of his *Memoir of the Author of A Vindication of the Rights of Women*. Feminism was associated with Saint-Simonianism during the early years of the nineteenth century; see Taylor, passim.

[4] Seven Cambridge undergraduates tell Ida's story; the listening women provide the interpolated lyrics.

[5] She was careful to place the Bedford College Trust in the hands of single women before she died, according to Levine (*VF* 32).

[6] Herstein 53. In 1869 Josephine Butler could still write of middle-class women: "to say they can be educated at home, under mothers who are themselves uneducated, is to offer a stone to those who ask bread" (xx).

[7] Dating the Woodard Foundation schools accurately is difficult because of their various moves and transformations (Heeney, *Mission* passim); the dates given in the text mark significant moves towards their final identity.

[8] An affectionate version of Miss Dyson is the playfully named Miss Lyveson of *Pillars*, who "had devoted herself to educating children of better birth than means" (1.78), such as little Robina Underwood. Miss Lyveson's school is at Catsacre, Miss Dyson's school at Dogmersfield.

[9] Throughout her life Yonge was involved directly in education. Soon after her birth her mother founded a village school paid for by Yonge's grandmother, and from earliest girlhood to old age Yonge taught in the Sunday School. At least 67 of the items listed in Battiscombe and Laski's bibliography are intended for school use, such as the Scripture Readings for Schools series, the Landmarks of History series, and the Cameos from English History series.

[10] In *Womankind* Yonge asserts that girls of fifteen can appear "far superior" to brothers of the same age, but that intrinsic male superiority will be seen from the fact that a boy will learn more in one vacation than a girl does in a year or two: "But she thinks and reflects more" (*Womankind* 69). Yet Ethel is shown as able to keep up with her older brother and occasionally overtake him, despite the many other things that as a girl she must do.

[11] References to *Aurora Leigh* provide first the page number in McSweeney's edition, then the book number and line number. Marjorie Stone comments on this passage that "inverting a well-known classical image of gender inversion, Barrett Browning subverts the traditional focus of the epic on male heroic exploits through a doubly transvestite simile relating Achilles . . . to a young girl and her education." She goes on to note that Browning's wrestling metaphor and the comparison of the young Aurora to the young Achilles suggest that the education Aurora's father gives her is wholly male. In fact, however, the poem constantly emphasizes that "the most vital thing he teaches her is . . . the importance of Love" (117). The same might be said

of Dr. May whose nurturing side is emphasized in all the novels in which he features. However, for the purposes of my argument the important point is that for both girls a narrow and unexciting education is equated with an old-fashioned and unsympathetic woman (Aurora's Aunt and Miss Winter), while their classical education is equated with an intelligent and sympathetic male (Aurora's father and Norman May).

[12] The sensible Flora May recognizes that Miss Winter's questions are "great nonsense" (85), but they are not challenged because she is a reliable guide to manners and morals. As with Cherry Elwood her old-fashioned liabilities in some ways function as assets.

[13] She first writes in imitation of the poets found among her father's books (32-33; 1.971-1002).

[14] Ethel means reading aloud; she suffers considerably from having to listen to her unintelligent sister Mary reading Shakespeare (she "murders" the quarrel scene in *Julius Caesar*, according to Ethel [65]). Yonge, however, places reading aloud as the first priority in a woman's education (*Womankind* 39) presumably because it was useful in entertaining the rest of the family.

[15] Meta's father is made uncomfortable by the change in her appearance when she is dressed by a housemaid rather than her lady's maid.

[16] Later this point is reinforced by a comparison between the Wards' drawing room and that of the Mays, "so decidedly for use and not for show" (*The Trial* 29). Elizabeth Gaskell also uses a comparison between the drawing rooms of two families to suggest different ideas of the relation between gentility and usefulness: in *North and South* the Hales' drawing room is full of signs of employment, while the Thornes' is clearly kept merely for show. Tristram points this out and adds "the lived-in look can of course be fabricated. Loudon [of the influential *Loudon's Encyclopaedia of Cottage, Farm, and Villa Architecture*, 1833], who feels that the appearance of idleness makes rooms look dismal, suggests how the slothful may counterfeit employment: 'This effect would be produced by the daily papers, and some periodical works, and open letters received in the morning on the principal tables; and on other tables, some of the blotting-books might be open: the inkstands not thoroughly in order, with some unfinished writing and open books or portfolios would give at least the appearance of industry'" (187). This look is clearly what Yonge regards as desirable, judging from the interiors in her novels: see, for instance, *The Heir of Redclyffe*, which is especially full of charming cluttered interiors.

[17] Dennis notes that Yonge's gardener's younger daughter was made a pupil teacher in a local school and eventually sent to Shrewsbury Training College for training as a school mistress (26).

[18] Not only the Tractarians showed this concern for changes in the public schools, although as a group they were especially active. Thomas Arnold of Rugby was the best-known educational reformer for many years, especially in the 1830s.

[19] Nina Auerbach writes of the effects on the movement to improve women's education of the distaste at the idea of girls in continued close contact with each other (14-15). She points out that Mary Wollstonecraft in *A Vindication of the Rights of*

Women also objected strongly to "many females being shut up together in nurseries, schools, or convents."

[20] Some measure of the extent to which Yonge's views about communities of women changed is provided by her consenting with pleasure to the founding in July, 1899, of the Charlotte Yonge scholarship—a scholarship in her honour awarded every other year to a girl from Winchester High School going to university (Battiscombe, *Yonge* 161).

[21] Yonge's suspicions of institutions as such are shared by more liberal contemporaries, such as Josephine Butler, who argues that "everything worked on the elastic and varied principle of home life thrives far better than the costliest institution. . . . Everything lives and thrives better where there is the principle of play and freedom which home affords and which is necessarily excluded where rule prevails, as it must do in enormous institutions" (xxxviii).

[22] Mrs. May is dubious about his ambitions, as suggested by the letter read after her death (49).

NOTES TO CHAPTER TWO

[1] Ford Madox Brown worked on his key painting *Work* (Manchester City Art Gallery) from 1852-65; the painting includes the figure of Carlyle, whose ideas about the role of work in society as expressed in *Past and Present* are central to this painting and to most mid-nineteenth-century discussions of the subject (Treuherz 87).

[2] Butler here is writing more specifically about lower middle-class women and a way of life that she sees as leading to possible seduction and eventual prostitution.

[3] When Emmeline in *The Castle Builders* (1850) is disillusioned with religion, her clergyman brother-in-law asks her pointedly: "You tried to feel. What did you try to do?" (290).

[4] Showalter's introductory remarks to Dinah Mulock Craik's *On Sisterhoods* emphasize the labour involved: she quotes Vicinus on the "rigorous regimen" of the sisterhoods and refers to the experiences of one of the early sisters, Margaret Goodman, who states that "the work is far too real to be performed by lagging hands" (268).

[5] I am grateful to Susan Mumm for permission to read an extended version of her unpublished paper, "Stolen Daughters, Virgin Mothers: the Nun as Cultural Threat in Victorian Britain," which helped me to correct some overgeneralizations on the subject of the nineteenth-century Anglican orders for women. Mumm lists eight common reasons for opposition to the sisterhoods.

[6] *Suggestions for Thought for Seekers after Religious Truth among the Artisans of England* (London, Eyre and Spottiswood, for private circulation 1860) 2.225; quoted by Mumm.

[7] Frances Power Cobbe was a notable exception, however; she consistently expressed a low opinion of religious orders, regarding convents as "the withering precincts" in which novices "are shrivelled from women into nuns" (14).

[8] Notably the Scobell case in Eastbourne, which Mumm discusses in some detail.

[9] Anthony Harrison discusses sisterhoods in relation to Christina Rossetti. See also Prelinger (188).

[10] For instance, in *The Young Stepmother*, Yonge's heroine, Albinia Kendal, marries partly for love but also partly because her three stepchildren will provide an outlet for her energies; even when her own children are born she still works tirelessly for charity and takes on the care of the invalid grandmother of her stepchildren.

[11] Elizabeth Blackwell was placed on the British Medical Register in 1859, the first woman to appear there (*VF* 96).

[12] Yonge's objection to women doctors seems to have survived until the end of her writing career. In *Modern Broods*, her last novel, Geraldine Grinstead (once Geraldine Underwood), one of the characters who is most likely to act as mouthpiece for her author, is represented as shuddering at the idea of part of the family estate being used for "a sort of convalescent or children's hospital for the training of women intending to study medicine or nursing" (262). The institution finally established does not, apparently, train women doctors.

[13] In the United States, Louisa May Alcott wrote novels for both adults and children that discuss women's work, such as *Work* (1872) and *An Old-Fashioned Girl* (1870).

[14] A few non-canonical women novelists of this period wrote about women and work, as for instance Margaret Oliphant did in *Kirsteen*, but this novel was not published until 1891.

[15] Yonge admired Austen: she and Elizabeth Wordsworth, the first Principal of Lady Margaret Hall, Oxford, held enjoyable discussions "capping Miss Austen *con amore*," and she refers directly in her novels to *Emma* (*Pillars* 2.347) as well as *Mansfield Park* (*Pillars* 2.6) and *Persuasion* (*Trial* 53).

[16] The Female Middle Class Emigration Society functioned from 1862-86; it helped 302 women to emigrate (Hammerton 53).

[17] According to Sandbach-Dahlstrom, Yonge's "erring heroine is treated with a good deal of sympathy" (164).

[18] Sandbach-Dahlstrom's epilogue discusses the mutilated figures found in Yonge's fiction.

[19] Dinah Mulock Craik voiced one of the rationalizations of the anxious Academicians, namely the question of propriety, saying that there is "a not unnatural repugnance" to women's drawing from the life, but that "many lower and yet honourable positions are open to women handlers of the brush" (84). Cherry's accuracy in figure drawing is favourably contrasted with Edgar's, however (2.33).

[20] Yonge's women writers include Ermine in *The Clever Woman of the Family*. Bessie Merrifield (in "Come to her Kingdom," *Two Sides of the Shield*, and *Modern Broods*) is a respected writer, and Arthurine Arthuret (also in "Come to her Kingdom" and *Modern Broods*) publishes articles in magazines and gives lectures. A letter of Yonge's records doing her editorial work by reading or having read aloud the submissions to *The Monthly Packet* in the drawing room with her mother and sister-in-law (Battiscombe, *Yonge* 114).

[21] This narrative is similar to the story of the founding of the community of St. John at Clewer: Mrs. Harriet Monsell devoted her life to charitable work in an attempt to recover from her grief at the death of her husband.

[22] Keble writes "it strikes me there is a particular danger to people situated as these Sisters are among us; viz., that being so very few and being among persons so

deeply interested in them and their undertaking, they may easily think too much of themselves" (Anson 238).

[23] Quoted by Nestor, 21. In fact, Brian Heeney points out that the sisterhoods were criticized as being too independent of the established pattern of ecclesiastical authority (*Movement* 66).

NOTES TO CHAPTER THREE

[1] The work calendar for *Is He Popenjoy?* (Sutherland, "Introduction" xxi) records that it was "begun 12 October 1874. Finished 3 May, 1875"; *The Three Brides* was serialized in *The Monthly Packet* from January 1874 to June 1876.

[2] Holcombe's book and article are essential studies of the subject of the reform of married women's property law.

[3] As opposed to equity: wealthy families arranged marriage settlements to protect women and children.

[4] E.g., *English Laws for Women in the Nineteenth Century* (1854) and *The "Non-Existence" of Women* (1855).

[5] In her last novel, *Modern Broods*, Yonge uses as a chapter title "The Regiment of Women"; the very different implications of the phrase in the later work, where it heads a discussion of women's achievements at a school prize day, can be gathered from the epigraph to the chapter: "And happier than the merriest games / Is the joy of our new and nobler aims" (146).

[6] Cobbe groups "the types of Woman considered as an Adjective" as domestic, social, wife, mother, housewife, companion, plaything, or idol. "The types of Woman, considered as a Noun" are firstly the woman who makes her own happiness her end, and finally, the type whose example Cobbe advocates—the woman who makes "Virtue and Religion her end" (6-7).

[7] Quite credibly, too, as the number of intelligent and educated women who opposed women's causes demonstrates.

[8] The dead father's family name was Charnock. Because the mother, a Poynsett, inherited her family estate, she takes the name of her own family, too, and is known as Mrs. Charnock Poynsett. The heir to the estate (first Raymond, then Miles) is known as Mr. Charnock Poynsett; his brothers are just Charnocks.

[9] Trollope's sympathy with the suffering caused by the contemporary position of women, shown especially in his other (and far greater) novels of this period (Hall 339-40; Kincaid 291; McMaster 161, 179), such as *He Knew He Was Right* (1869), or *Phineas Finn* (1869), as well as in some of his letters, never extended to feminist activism (Kincaid 153-54; McMaster 179).

[10] Her behaviour, however, bears more resemblance to that of Aurora Floyd, the heroine of Mary Braddon's sensation novel of the same name (1862), who eloped with a groom.

[11] Sandbach-Dahlstrom sees Bessie herself as diabolical (147).

[12] Her married name is also presumably chosen because of its negative associations: Lord Tyrrel organized the murder of the little princes in the tower, according to Shakespeare's *Richard III*.

117

[13] A similar image is used in *Womankind* where Yonge deplores any need for women to guard themselves: "where there has been need of defence, there comes a hardening; and that delicate bloom of perfect modesty must needs be rubbed off" (105).

[14] In her last novel, *Modern Broods*, two young women, talking about "the great future opened to women," speak of "modesty and womanliness and retiring" and agree "we shall never do any good without it" (152-55).

[15] Battiscombe and Laski list nine educational books for young children with "Aunt Charlotte" titles between 1873 and 1883 (205-206); all are history books apart from *Aunt Charlotte's Evenings at Home with the Poets* (Aunt Charlotte at home with Byron?) and *Aunt Charlotte's Scripture Readings*.

NOTES TO EPILOGUE

[1] Sandbach-Dahlstrom sees characters like Mr. Clare and Alick Keith (in *The Clever Woman of the Family*) and Felix Underwood as "not the common run of man . . . but idealized projections of a woman's dreams of what men could be if they adopted female virtues" (167). While this is a tenable argument, it does not explain adequately how such characters function in Yonge's novels.

[2] Another striking example of a novel with a feminized hero is *Dynevor Terrace* (1857). Louis, Viscount Fitzjocelyn is described as strongly resembling his dead mother and as naturally endowed with feminine virtues—"gentleness, affection, humility, refinement" (470). Although religion is said to have "made a man of Louis," (470), it makes a man of him through other virtues traditionally associated with the female—"duty, submission and love" (470). Sandbach-Dahlstrom, writing of her male characters, describes Yonge as offering "a vision of an ideal androgynous community ruled by the Christian values that women have often made their own" (7); while my readings of the texts differ considerably from Sandbach-Dahlstrom's, we are evidently addressing the same phenomena.

[3] See for instance Mermin's "Heroic Sisterhood," which discusses "Goblin Market" but also refers to another Rossetti poem, "From House to House," and to Florence Nightingale's *Cassandra* (112). In *Aurora Leigh* the suffering innocent, Marian Erle, is identified by implication with Christ (see, for instance, 110; 3.1220-24, 110; 3.1227-28, 222; 6.1271-74, and 305; 9.250-51).

[4] Sandbach-Dahlstrom provides a useful summary of the plot, read simply in terms of Romance: "A young knight (baronet), Guy Morville, over whom a curse is hanging, is forced to leave his ancestral home on the death of his grandfather. He seeks sanctuary at Hollywell, where he meets a young damsel, Amabel (Amy) whom he asks to become his lady. Separated from her by the machinations of his arch enemy and the latter's sister . . . Guy descends from the ideal world of Hollywell into a lower world. . . . He suffers a period of spiritual trial and temptation, performs deeds of valour, and is rewarded by being reunited with his lady. They marry, but as Guy's spiritual quest has been completed, he dies and ascends to the world of the angels" (30).

5 In the case of both Amy's marriage to Guy and Laura's to Philip, the change in general family relationships is presented as being as important as the private relationship. I would argue that while Yonge usually imagines marriage in terms of the husband becoming part of the wife's family, as she does here in *The Heir of Redclyffe* and also in *The Pillars of the House*, her traditional views on gender relations lead her to advocate that the wife become part of the husband's family.

6 Amy's brother Charles also describes her in these terms, but while he belittles her affectionately, Philip believes that "she is a mere child, and will hardly ever be anything very more; but she is a very good little amiable thing" (227).

7 Sandbach-Dahlstrom speaks of Yonge's constant references in *The Heir of Redclyffe* to the importance of reading, including novel-reading, to the moral life.

8 See Sandbach-Dahlstrom (50) and Coleridge (175).

9 The Underwoods are rewarded for their virtues by having the family estate restored to them in a properly romantic fashion; Felix, like Guy, suffers in some sense as a scapegoat for a family sin of sacrilege (Guy's ancestor committed murder in Canterbury cathedral, Felix's ancestors prospered from lands sequestered from the church at the Reformation). However, on the whole the narrative avoids the romantic paradigms exploited so successfully in *The Heir of Redclyffe*.

10 Their father dies at this stage, their mother three years later. However, as their mother has had an accident which leaves her mentally ill they are "almost worse than orphans" (1.68) at this stage.

11 Battiscombe (*Keble* 70) argues that the care of a parish was his main concern but makes it clear that care of his father was also a prime motive. Keble's sense of filial duty is also obvious in his decision to publish *The Christian Year*, which he says happened "only in obedience to my father's wishes" (Battiscombe, *Keble* 104).

12 Exceptions appear in the late Merrifield-Mohun sequences (*The Two Sides of the Shield, Beechcroft at Rockstone, The Long Vacation, Modern Broods*), where her domineering soldierly males conform to patriarchal stereotypes.

13 Mrs. Edmonstone quotes this hymn when talking to Guy about his social responsibilities.

14 The "tales" referred to here are *Abbey Church, Scenes and Characters, The Castle Builders, Henrietta's Wish*, and *The Two Guardians*.

15 "The Author of Heartsease and Modern Schools of Fiction," *The Perspective Review* 10 (1854): 461; quoted by Sandbach-Dahlstrom (17).

WORKS CITED

Allchin, A. M. *The Silent Rebellion: Anglican Religious Communities 1845-1900.* London: SCM Press, 1958.

Anson, Peter F. *The Call of the Cloister: Religious Communities and Kindred Bodies in the Anglican Communion.* London: SPCK, 1964.

Armstrong, Nancy. *Desire and Domestic Fiction: A Political History of the Novel.* Oxford: Oxford UP, 1987.

Auerbach, Nina. *Communities of Women: An Idea in Fiction.* Cambridge: Harvard UP, 1978.

Battiscombe, Georgina. *Charlotte Mary Yonge: The Story of an Uneventful Life.* London: Constable, 1944.

———. *John Keble: A Study in Limitations.* New York: Alfred A. Knopf, 1964.

——— and Marghanita Laski, eds. *A Chaplet for Charlotte Yonge: Papers by Georgina Battiscombe [and Others].* London: Cresset, 1965.

Bauer, Carol and Lawrence Ritt. *Free and Ennobled: Source Readings in the Development of Victorian Feminism.* Oxford: Pergamon Press, 1979.

Beer, Gillian. *George Eliot.* Brighton: Harvester, 1986.

Blake, Kathleen. "*Middlemarch* and the Woman Question." *Nineteenth Century Fiction* 31 (1976): 285-312.

Brontë, Charlotte. *Shirley: A Tale.* Harmondsworth: Penguin, 1968.

Brown, Susan. "A Victorian Sappho: Agency, Identity, and the Politics of Poetics." *English Studies in Canada* 20 (1994): 205-26.

Burstyn, Joan N. *Victorian Education and the Ideal of Womanhood.* Totowa, New Jersey: Barnes and Noble, 1980.

Butler, Josephine. "Introduction." *Women's Work and Women's Culture: A Series of Essays.* Ed. Josephine Butler. London: Macmillan and Co., 1869. vii-lxiv.

Byatt, A. S. *Possession: A Romance.* London: Chatto & Windus, 1990.

Casteras, Susan B. "Virgin Vows: The Early Victorian Artists' Portrayal of Nuns and Novices." *Victorian Studies* 24 (1981): 157-84.

Church, R. W. *The Oxford Movement: Twelve Years, 1833-1845.* London: Archon Books, 1966.

Cobbe, Frances Power. "The Final Cause of Women." *Women's Work and Women's Culture: A Series of Essays.* Ed. Josephine Butler. London: Macmillan and Co., 1869. 1-26.

Coleridge, Christabel. *Charlotte Mary Yonge: Her Life and Letters.* Detroit: Gale, 1969.

Craik, Dinah Mulock. "On Sisterhoods" and "A Woman's Thoughts about Women." *Christina Rossetti "Maude," Dinah Mulock Craik "On Sisterhoods" and "A Woman's Thoughts about Women."* Ed. Elaine Showalter. London: William Pickering, 1993.

Davies, Emily. *Thoughts on Some Questions Relating to Women, 1860-1910.* New York: Kray Reprints, 1971.

Dennis, Barbara. *Charlotte Yonge (1823-1901), Novelist of the Oxford Movement.* Lewiston, NY: Edwin Mellen, 1992.

Dickens, Charles. *Uncollected Writings from Household Words 1850-59.* 2 vols. Ed. Harry Stone. Bloomington: Indiana UP, 1968.

Eliot, George. "Silly Novels by Lady Novelists." In *Selected Critical Writings.* Ed. Rosemary Ashton. Oxford: Oxford UP, 1992. 296-321.

Flint, Kate. "Introduction." *Can You Forgive Her?* By Anthony Trollope. Oxford: Oxford UP, 1982.

———. *The Woman Reader 1837-1914.* Oxford: Clarendon P, 1993.

Foster, Shirley. "Unpublished Letters of C. M. Yonge." *Notes and Queries* ns 17 (1970): 339-41.

Graver, Suzanne. *George Eliot and Community: A Study in Social Theory and Fictional Form.* Berkeley: U of California P, 1984.

Hall, N. John. *Trollope, A Biography.* Oxford: Clarendon P, 1992.

Hammerton, A. James. "Feminism and Female Emigration, 1861-1886." *A Widening Sphere: Changing Roles of Victorian Women.* Ed. Martha Vicinus. Bloomington, Indiana UP, 1977. 52-71.

Harman, Barbara Leah. "In Promiscuous Company: Female Public Appearance in Elizabeth Gaskell's *North and South.*" *Victorian Studies* 31 (1988): 351-74.

Harrison, Anthony H. "Christina Rossetti and the Sage Discourse of Feminist High Anglicanism." *Victorian Sages and Cultural Discourse: Renegotiating Gender and Power.* Ed. Thais E. Morgan. New Brunswick: Rutgers UP, 1990. 87-104.

Harrison, Brian H. *Separate Spheres: The Opposition to Women's Suffrage in Britain.* London: Croom Helm, 1978.

Hayter, Alethea. "The Sanitary Idea and a Victorian Novelist." *History Today* 19 (1969): 840-47.

Heeney, Brian. *Mission to the Middle Classes: The Woodard Schools, 1848-1891.* London: SPCK, 1969.

———. *The Women's Movement in the Church of England, 1850-1930.* Oxford: Clarendon P, 1988.

Heilbrun, Carolyn. *Reinventing Womanhood.* New York: Norton, 1979.

Helsinger, Elizabeth K., Robin Lauterbach Sheets, William Veeder. *The Woman Question: Defining Voices, 1837-1883.* Vol 1. New York: Garland, 1983.

Herstein, Sheila R. *A Mid-Victorian Feminist, Barbara Leigh Smith Bodichon.* New Haven: Yale UP, 1985.

Holcombe, Lee. "Victorian Wives and Property: Reform of the Married Women's Property Law, 1857-1882." *A Widening Sphere: Changing Roles of Victorian Women.* Ed. Martha Vicinus. Bloomington: Indiana UP, 1977. 3-28.

121

————. *Wives and Property: Reform of the Married Women's Property Law in Nineteenth Century England.* Toronto: U of Toronto P, 1983.

Hollis, Patricia. *Ladies Elect: Women in Local Government 1865-1914.* Oxford: Clarendon P, 1987.

Jameson, Anna. *Sisters of Charity, Catholic and Protestant and the Communion of Labour.* Boston: Ticknor and Fields, 1857.

Janes, Regina M. "On the Reception of *A Vindication of the Rights of Women.*" *Journal of the History of Ideas* 39 (1978): 293-302.

Jay, Elisabeth, ed. *Evangelicals and Tractarians.* Cambridge: Cambridge UP, 1983.

Keble, John. *The Christian Year: Thoughts in Verse for the Sundays and Holydays throughout the Year.* London: Church Literature Association, 1977.

Killham, John. *Tennyson and "The Princess": Reflections of an Age.* London: Athlone P, 1958.

Kincaid, James R. *The Novels of Anthony Trollope.* Oxford: Clarendon P, 1977.

Kowaleski-Wallace, Elizabeth. *Their Fathers' Daughters: Hannah More, Maria Edgeworth, and Patriarchal Complicity.* New York: Oxford UP, 1991.

Krueger, Christine L. *The Reader's Repentance: Women Preachers, Women Writers, and Nineteenth Century Social Discourse.* Chicago: U of Chicago P, 1992.

Langland, Elizabeth. *Anne Brontë: The Other One.* Basingstoke: Macmillan Education, 1989.

Leighton, Angela. *Victorian Women Poets: Writing Against the Heart.* Charlottesville: UP of Virginia, 1992.

Levine, Philippa. *Victorian Feminism 1850-1900.* London: Hutchinson, 1987.

————. *Feminist Lives in Victorian England: Private Roles and Public Commitment.* Oxford: Basil Blackwell, 1990.

McGann, Jerome J. "Introduction." *The Achievement of Christina Rossetti.* Ed. David A. Kent. Ithaca: Cornell UP, 1987. 1-19.

McMaster, Juliet. *Trollope's Palliser Novels: Theme and Pattern.* London: Macmillan, 1978.

McSweeney, Kevin. "Introduction." *Aurora Leigh.* By Elizabeth Barrett Browning. Oxford: Oxford UP, 1993.

Mare, Margaret and Alicia C. Percival. *Victorian Best-seller: The World of Charlotte M. Yonge.* London: Harrap, 1947.

Mellor, Anne K. *Romanticism and Gender.* New York: Routledge, 1993.

Mermin, Dorothy. "Heroic Sisterhood in *Goblin Market.*" *Victorian Poetry* 21 (1983): 107-18.

————. *Godiva's Ride: Women of Letters in England, 1830-1880.* Bloomington: Indiana UP, 1993.

Mill, John Stuart. *The Subjection of Women.* New York: Frederick A. Stokes, 1911.

Mumm, Susan. "Stolen Daughters, Virgin Mothers: The Nun as Cultural Threat in Victorian Britain." Unpublished paper presented to the Victorian Studies Association of Western Canada Conference, Vancouver, October 1994.

Nestor, Pauline. *Female Friendships and Communities: Charlotte Brontë, George Eliot, Elizabeth Gaskell.* Oxford: Clarendon P, 1985.

Newman, John Henry. [*Apologia Pro Vita Sua*] *A History of My Religious Opinions. Newman: Prose and Poetry.* Ed. G. Tillotson. London: Rupert Hart-Davis, 1957. 569-789.

Nightingale, Florence. *Cassandra: An Essay.* Ed. Myra Starck. Old Westbury, NY: Feminist Press, 1979.

Nunn, Pamela Gerrish. *Victorian Women Artists.* London: Woman's P, 1987.

Ollard, S. L. *A Short History of the Oxford Movement.* London: Mowbray, 1983.

Pedersen, Joyce Senders. "Some Victorian Headmistresses: A Conservative Tradition of Social Reform." *Victorian Studies* 24 (1981): 463-84.

Poovey, Mary. *Uneven Developments: The Ideological Work of Gender in Mid-Victorian England.* Chicago: U of Chicago P, 1988.

Prelinger, Catherine M. "The Female Diaconate in the Anglican Church: What Kind of Ministry for Women?" *Religion in the Lives of English Women 1760-1930.* Ed. Gail Malmgreem. London: Croom Helm, 1986. 161-92.

Prickett, Stephen. "Romantics and Victorians: From Typology to Symbolism." *Reading the Text: Biblical Criticism and Literary Theory.* Ed. Stephen Prickett. Oxford: Blackwell's, 1991. 182-224.

Pugh, Martin. *Women's Suffrage in Britain: 1867-1928.* London: Historical Association, 1980.

Reed, John Shelton. "A Female Movement: The Feminization of Nineteenth-Century Anglo-Catholicism." *Anglican and Episcopal History* 57 (1988): 199-238.

Rendall, Jane. *The Origins of Modern Feminism: Women in Britain, France and the United States, 1780-1860.* London: Macmillan Education, 1985.

Romanes, Ethel. *Charlotte Mary Yonge: An Appreciation.* London: Mowbray, 1908.

Rossetti, Christina. "Maude." *Christina Rossetti "Maude," Dinah Mulock Craik "On Sisterhoods" and "A Woman's Thoughts about Women."* Ed. Elaine Showalter. London: William Pickering, 1993.

Rover, Constance. *Women's Suffrage and Party Politics in Britain 1866-1914.* London: Routledge and Kegan Paul, 1967.

Rowbotham, Judith. *Good Girls Make Good Wives: Guidance for Girls in Nineteenth Century Fiction.* Oxford: Blackwell's, 1989.

Sandbach-Dahlstrom, Catherine. *Be Good Sweet Maid: Charlotte Yonge's Domestic Fiction: A Study in Dogmatic Purpose and Fictional Form.* Stockholm: Almqvist & Wicksell, 1984.

Schor, Naomi. *Reading in Detail: Aesthetics and the Feminine.* New York: Methuen, 1987.

Showalter, Elaine. *A Literature of Their Own: British Women Novelists from Brontë to Lessing.* Princeton: Princeton UP, 1977.

——, ed. *Christina Rossetti "Maude," Dinah Mulock Craik "On Sisterhoods" and "A Woman's Thoughts about Women."* London: William Pickering, 1993.

Spencer, Jane. *The Rise of the Woman Novelist: From Aphra Behn to Jane Austen.* Oxford: Basil Blackwell, 1986.

Stone, Marjorie. "Genre Subversion and Gender Inversion: *The Princess* and *Aurora Leigh.*" *Victorian Poetry* 25 (1987): 101-27.

Strachey, Ray. *"The Cause": A Short History of the Women's Movement in Great Britain.* Port Washington, NY: Kennikat P, 1969.

Sutherland, John. "Introduction." *Is He Popenjoy?* By Anthony Trollope. Oxford: Oxford UP, 1986.

———. *Mrs. Humphry Ward: Eminent Victorian, Pre-eminent Edwardian.* Oxford: Oxford UP, 1991.

Taylor, Barbara. *Eve and the New Jerusalem: Socialism and Feminism in the Nineteenth Century.* London: Virago, 1988.

Tennyson, Alfred. *The Princess. Tennyson: A Selected Edition.* Ed. Christopher Ricks. London: Longman, 1989. 219-330.

Thompson, Nicola. "Gender and the Reception of Victorian Novels: Emily Brontë's *Wuthering Heights,* Anthony Trollope's *Barchester Towers,* Charles Reade's *It is Never Too Late to Mend,* Charlotte Yonge's *The Heir of Redclyffe.*" Diss., Emory U, 1992.

Treuherz, Julian. *Victorian Painting.* London: Thames and Hudson, 1993.

Tristram, Philippa. *Living Space in Fact and Fiction.* London: Routledge, 1989.

Trollope, Anthony. "The Higher Education of Women." *Four Essays.* Ed. Morris C. Parrish. London, 1938.

Tuchman, Gaye. *Edging Women Out: Victorian Novelists, Publishers, and Social Change.* New Haven: Yale UP, 1989.

Vicinus, Martha. *Independent Women: Work and Community for Single Women, 1850-1920.* Chicago: U of Chicago P, 1985.

Walkowitz, Judith. *Prostitution and Victorian Society: Women, Class, and the State.* Cambridge: Cambridge UP, 1980.

*Yonge, Charlotte Mary. *The Castle Builders: Or the Deferred Confirmation.* London: J. and C. Mozeley, 1859.

———. *The Two Guardians: or, Home in this World.* London: J. Masters, 1874.

———. *The Heir of Redclyffe.* London: Macmillan and Co., 1880.

———. *The Daisy Chain, or Aspirations: A Family Chronicle.* London: Virago, 1988.

———. *Heartsease, or The Brother's Wife.* London: Macmillan and Co., 1893.

———. *Dynevor Terrace: or, The Clue of Life.* London: Macmillan and Co., 1908.

———. "Last Heartsease Leaves." *A Chaplet for Charlotte Yonge.* Ed. Battiscombe and Laski. London: Cresset, 1965. 128-38.

———. *The Clever Woman of the Family.* London: Virago, 1985.

———. *The Trial or, More Links in the Daisy Chain.* London: Macmillan and Co., 1914.

———. "A Link Between *The Castle Builders* and *The Pillars of the House.*" *A Chaplet for Charlotte Yonge.* Ed. Battiscombe and Laski. London: Cresset, 1965. 139-51.

———. "Children's Literature of the Last Century: Didactic Fiction." *Macmillan's Magazine* 1869, 310.

———. *Musings over "The Christian Year" and "Lyra Innocentium" Together with a Few Gleanings of Recollections of the Rev. J. Keble.* London: Macmillan and Co., 1871.

———. *The Pillars of the House: or, Under Wode, Under Rode.* 2 vols. London: Macmillan and Co., 1889.

———. *Aunt Charlotte's Stories of English History for the Little Ones.* London: Marcus Ward, 1873.

———. *The Three Brides.* London: Macmillan and Co., 1876.

———. *Womankind.* London: Mozeley and Smith, 1877.

———. *The Two Sides of the Shield.* 2 vols. London: Macmillan and Co., 1885.

———. " A Review of Nieces." *More Bye-Words.* London: Macmillan and Co., 1890. 123-187.

———. *An Old Woman's Outlook in a Hampshire Village.* London: Macmillan and Co., 1892.

———. "Authorship." *A Chaplet For Charlotte Yonge.* Ed. Battiscombe and Laski. London: Cresset, 1965. 185-92.

———. "Lifelong Friends." *A Chaplet For Charlotte Yonge.* Ed. Battiscombe and Laski. London: Cresset, 1965. 181-84.

———. *The Long Vacation.* London: Macmillan and Co., 1895.

———. *John Keble's Parishes: A History of Hursley and Otterbourne.* London: Macmillan and Co., 1898.

———. *Modern Broods, or, Developments Unlooked-For.* London: Macmillan and Co., 1900.

* There are no standard editions of any of Yonge's works. Virago published reprints of *The Daisy Chain* and *The Clever Woman of the Family* in the 1980s. My references are drawn from the editions available to me through my own collection or through the libraries to which I have had access. Yonge's works are listed here in the order in which they were originally published as books.

ENGLISH LITERARY STUDIES MONOGRAPH SERIES